BEYOND THE FOREST GARDEN

Robert A de J Hart

BEYOND THE FOREST GARDEN

Robert A de J Hart

Gaia Books Limited

A GAIA ORIGINAL

Books from Gaia celebrate the vision of Gaia, the self-sustaining living Earth, and seek to help readers live in greater personal and planetary harmony.

Editorial	Charlie Ryrie
Design and Illustration	Lucy Guenot
Managing Editor	Pip Morgan
Production	Susan Walby

First published in the United Kingdom in 1996 by
Gaia Books Ltd, 66 Charlotte Street, London W1P 1LR
and 20 High Street Stroud, Glos GL5 1AS.

ISBN 1-85675-037-X

A catalogue record of this book is available from the British Library.

Printed and bound in the UK by Hillman Printers
through Amon Re Ltd.

This paper is 100% recycled using a non-bleach
and non-de-inking process.

10 9 8 7 6 5 4 3 2 1

For GDH: undying love

Contents

Preface

When the philosopher Plato returned to Athens from far flung voyages of exile and discovery following the death of his teacher, Socrates, he founded the Academy. He founded it not in the bustling city streets of the capital itself, but in a quiet forest grove beyond the city walls. This foundation was meant as a place of quiet contemplation, inspiration and study, devoted to the worship of the nine Muses, who inspired all the learned arts and sciences. Crucially, then, we can see that the initial foundation – from which all subsequent Academic institutions ultimately derive inspiration – began in a Forest Garden.

Through a series of publications over the years, and above all in his constant practice of a genuinely ecological lifestyle, Robert Hart has contributed greatly to the recovery of the lost meanings embodied in that original academic mission at its most profound. He is a unique living exemplar of the Forest Garden school of thought, an academic of the woods. We should listen to what he says, watch what he practises, and treasure him.

The significance of the tree is both metaphysical and physical. All the ancient teaching systems of spiritual wisdom allot a central role to the tree. The

8

PREFACE

Tree of Life is at the very heart of Jewish mystical thought in the Kabbalah, the very image of the deity in which we ourselves are fashioned. In Christianity the tree is at the centre of the cosmic drama of redemption. In Islam, Zoroastrianism and Hinduism; in Buddhist, Jain, Bahai and primal traditions, the tree is a primordial image of the utterly reliable and the transcendental, the Real.

Robert has spent a great deal of his life very close to trees, living with them, learning from them, and uncovering their enormous potential to assist and help humankind solve its complex social and ecological problems. In this new work, he has given his readers the gift of a series of semi poetic explorations of linked themes concerning the wider philosophical and spiritual dimensions of his life's work to date. Robert ranges far and wide in his meditations: he reconciles Christian and pagan traditions, ancient and contemporary beliefs; Gandhian influences; a reverence for place and people; Buddhist teachings on compassion; Tolstoy; yoga; literary and musical criticism and the wisdom of the feminine. He also provides practical ecological advice, interspersed with signposts for the spiritual path.

Again and again he comes back to the central theme of his life's work, like a great solid tree trunk from which radiate out the various branches of his thought and practice: the ways and powers of love.

Love, *caritas*, compassion, *agape*: it is this which infuses his thinking and gives it an invisible unity. Robert has struggled all his life against entropy, against illness, and against "the system". He has been able to overcome his struggles, and continue his journey, because he is buoyed up with a deep and implicit knowledge of the mysterious power of Love. He knows from his study of life, that love alone has the power to give ordered form and meaning, to bring healing, to share hope, to radiate clarity and beauty, and above all to generate life.

Others may write longer scientific texts on ecology, or more densely argued philosophical treatises littered with footnotes, but with Robert we are on surer ground than that. We are invited to travel briefly with a Master who has lived his philosophy. We are invited to walk for a while with him in the forest groves of the original Academy, and to learn about ourselves and our ideal destiny, should we be able to listen and claim it for our own.

The English word "book" comes from the old-English word "boc", meaning "a beech tree", as the earliest books written by our ancestors were engraved with runes on boards of beech wood. Such ancient works were sparse in outer lettering, but incredibly rich with inner meaning. In this sense, Robert's new work well deserves the ancient title. This book is the voice of his trees, speaking directly through him about the nature of the Real.

When you have finished Robert's work, go out into nature, to a garden or a park, and find a quiet grove of trees; become still, and allow yourself to open to their quiet presences. Only then will you begin to read the real meaning of this book, the next volume of which you yourself must compose with your own life, lived to its fullest glory.

Thomas Clough Daffern
International Institute of Peace Studies and Global Philosophy
December 1995

Prologue

The two strongest influences in my early life were two exceptionally loving women: my mother and grandmother. My mother was a highly gifted musician and linguist, as was my father, an international lawyer of Spanish Basque and Scots origin. They married solely because they wanted to be with each other, not from any desire for children. My mother was encouraged by her Italian singing master to become a dramatic soprano, but my parents were both people with an exceptional sense of responsibility which told them that a childless marriage was wrong. So my mother rejected the allure of an operatic career – to have me.

My birth was a near-disaster. I was born dead and my mother would have died if her mother had not alerted the doctor in time. Having just succeeded in reviving me, the doctor and nurse rushed to my mother's bed to resuscitate her. In the course of this process, my mother and myself both suffered shoulder injuries from which we never recovered. These contributed somehow to the tremendously strong bond between us. I was a delicate, sensitive and highly strung child, in constant pain and with very poor circulation so that I suffered agonies of cold in winter and was prostrated by heat in summer.

My grandmother was an earnest Christian funda-
mentalist. From her I acquired a love of the Bible and
a conviction that the miracles could be repeated in
the modern world if people were precise in obeying
spiritual laws. I resolved early on to try and discover
the Laws of Love, which I believed to be the basic
laws of life, and resolved to try and apply them to my
own and my family's problems. At about the age of
nine, I read the words: "With God, all things are possible". My reaction was: "If these words are true, then
I, as a weak and delicate child, can climb Everest."
My whole life has been an Everest ascent.

At that time my parents had just had their second
child, my brother Antony. His birth was truly a
disaster. He was born with a brain defect, which
meant that he was unable to speak, and which
impeded his development in other ways. A kind
Scots doctor told my mother: "We are unable to do
anything for him, and he probably won't survive
puberty. Take him home and give him all the love
you can." This she did, for the rest of her life. She
refused to accept the doctor's verdict, and made
untiring efforts to find means of healing or alleviating his condition. Her life became a saga of
heroic self-sacrifice.

My brother, who could have lived a short and
miserable life in an institution, was to lead a
reasonably long, happy, healthy and fulfilled life,
thanks to the efforts of my mother and myself. I
adored my mother for her courage and devotion.

Following my father's death, after a period spent as a journalist and on military service, I left London with my brother and mother and settled in the country, first in Norfolk, later in Somerset, and finally in my mother's ancestral county of Shropshire.

I had become a journalist through developing a keen interest in world affairs after studying the epic story of the Italian Risorgimento, while a pupil at Westminster School. I became particularly fascinated by the lives of national heroes such as Mazzini, Gandhi, and Kagawa, the Christian reformer known as the "Japanese Gandhi". From Gandhi I obtained the impelling vision of a world order, of which the basic unit would be the co-operative, democratic and largely self-sufficient rural community. From Kagawa one of the most important concepts I gained was the possibility of integrating conservation with food production by the growing of fodder bearing trees.

Deciding to specialise, as a writer, in the problem of world hunger, after a brief spell in Norfolk I bought an organic smallholding in a beautiful part of the Brendon Hills in West Somerset. I decided to farm for two equally important reasons, both to gain practical experience of food production, and in order to give my brother a useful and constructive life. I took up fruit growing, ferrying raspberries and black-currants over the Quantock Hills to a jam factory in Bridgwater. Later I moved to my present small farm on Wenlock Edge in Shropshire. There I took up cattle-rearing, to earn cash, and embarked on a self-sufficiency project so that I could provide fresh, wholesome produce for us all. This eventually led to the development of my Forest Garden, a concept which seems to have caught the imagination of people in many parts of the world.

The Forest Garden is part of a comprehensive way of life that I have developed, incorporating not only nutrition and work on the land, but also music and the disciplines of Raja Yoga. This way of life has been hugely beneficial to my health. My mother has also continued to play an important part in my life; even after her death she is very close to me.

My personal Everest climb is still continuing. Above all, at this critical period in the history of the world, I am seeking spiritual strength, comparable to that which led Gandhi to conceive the concept and technique of *Satyagraha* Holding to the Truth.

Wider Horizons

The Forest Garden project is a small, manmade ecosystem designed to integrate the principles of conservation and sustainable development. Its creation was the culmination of a long search to find a comprehensive answer to two closely related worldwide problems: large-scale degradation of the natural environment and the colossal toll of avoidable ill-health. It has been very exciting to watch the project develop over the years, and it is hugely rewarding to welcome visitors to my garden, and to meet so many vital, intelligent, and positive people who really give me hope for the future.

The project occupies a sheltered site on the western slopes of Wenlock Edge, in the beautiful and historical Welsh Border area of the English Midlands. It has aroused considerable interest in many parts of the world since it was first launched in the mid-1980s. Some of the many people who have visited it in recent years have seen in it a small model of a way of life, suitable for those who wish to confront and survive the infinitely pressing problems of this millennial era. Some have seen the garden as a symbol of the wider world herself, a world containing many worlds, each integrated with the others and working together for the good of the whole.

The garden combines practical and therapeutic qualities, and I hope it inspires others with its peaceful yet intensely productive potential. In this book I hope that I can explain in some way the importance of the Forest Garden, its place in the wider scheme of things, and the way that it is just one strand in the many streams of thought and practice that exist to lead and inspire us. Through my life I have found inspiration, joy, solace and therapy from many different sources. Positive influences surround us, if we only let ourselves care enough to listen.

There is evidence that the site of the Forest Garden was first inhabited by a hardy Celtic Christian pioneering community some time in the early centuries of the first millenium AD. A raised circular earthwork in the paddock above the present house is believed to mark the position of a Celtic

Christian "monestery" – a stockaded ring of family huts surrounding a small chapel.

Celtic Christianity was ideally suited to provide spiritual strength, inspiration, and guidance for women and men hewing out homes in the primeval forest. It combined the love-teachings of the New Testament, especially the Gospel of St John, with reverence for the Earth Mother, Gaia, who was known to the "pagan" Celts as Brigit and canonised by the church as St Bride. It therefore embraced both the moral rigour of Christ and the sense of compassion for the natural world inculcated by the maternal principle. In Chinese terms, it constituted a perfect balance between yang and yin. It also resembled other "ecological" religions, such as those of the American Indians. The well-known letter of Chief Seattle to the President of the United States expresses the profound conviction of the oneness of all life which was also part of the mystic inheritance of the Celtic Christians:

"Every part of the earth is sacred to my people, every shining pine needle, every sandy shore, every mist in the dark woods, every meadow, every humming insect. All are holy in the memory and instinct of my people. We know the sap which courses through the trees, as we know the blood which courses through our veins. We are part of the earth as the earth is part of us. The perfumed flowers are our sisters. The bear, the deer, the great eagle, these are our brothers."

In *The Elements of Celtic Christianity*[1] Anthony Duncan writes, "Celtic Christianity is essentially an embracing of life in its totality." Of the Christian faith that came to Britain, together with the other Mediterranean and Middle Eastern religions practised within the cosmopolitan ranks of the Roman army, he affirms: "It spoke of forgiveness, integrity and eternal life. It swept up the best of paganism in an all-fulfilling embrace, and revealed creation as the transfigured image of God."

According to tradition, Joseph of Arimathea was the first to bring Christianity to Britain following the Resurrection. He is said to have worked out the spot near Glastonbury which was destined to be the site of the first church, according to the age-old principles of geomancy, and to have indicated it by planting his staff in the earth. The staff then proceeded to take root and blossom – as tree cuttings tend to – and it became the Glastonbury Thorn.

I can't help wondering whether the Celtic Christian pioneers who occupied my own land used the same type of geomantic techniques to select the site of that settlement. No doubt one consideration that strongly influenced the choice was the spring of deliciously pure and highly mineralised water to the north of the house, which I still enjoy. This spring was regarded from an early time as a potent spot,

1. *The Elements of Celtic Christianity*, Anthony Duncan, Element Books, Shaftesbury, 1992

shown by the fact that it is a meeting place for four ancient trackways: a deeply indented prehistoric packhorse track, possibly a stone-axe trading route; a Roman road leading to a quarry which supplied roofing tiles for the city of Viroconium; a bridleway which goes to a remote hamlet called Middlehope which once boasted a Norman castle, and a pilgrims' way to the shrine at Much Wenlock, dedicated to St Milburga, a Saxon princess who was also a Celtic Christian prioress.

Below the house is a deep depression which is believed to have been a monastic fishpond, and the Forest Garden project[2] occupies an artificial promontory, which was presumably built up when the pond was dug out. Visitors often comment on the area's peaceful atmosphere, and I can't help attributing this to the potent influence of the old monks and nuns. I feel a warm sense of kinship for those courageous colonists, as well as for St Milburga, who probably first despatched them into the wilderness, and for Caractacus, the British chief whose hill-fort of Caer Caradoc I can just discern to the west. The house appears to be built upon a leyline connecting Caer Caradoc to another Iron Age hill-fort to the east, on Brown Clee hill.

The experimental area, or my Forest Garden project, comprises a number of sections: three small

2. *Forest Gardening*, Robert A de J Hart, Green Books, Bideford, UK, 1991, 2nd edition 1996

model forest gardens; a number of "forest clearings" designed for sun-loving vegetables and herbs which are essential if you want to ensure an adequate diet throughout the year; two reed-beds and two ponds for the benefit of moisture-loving plants, and to attract wild-life; two willow coppices, one cut for basketry and the other for shredding to supply materials for composting and mulching; an arboretum of specimen trees from every continent; and a circle-dancing area, surrounding the English oak dedicated to H. J. Massingham, the great country writer who was one of the first to inspire my organic ventures. There is also a log cabin expertly built by my gardener Garnet Jones to house guests, with a wind-generator to supply electric light, an organic loo, a waterwheel and a greenhouse.

From the first the Forest Garden was designed to be a sanctuary of health. It provides many basic essentials for the health and harmonious development of body, mind, soul, and spirit: pure water, pure air, pure food, a beautiful and stimulating environment, and conditions for constructive and creative exercise, utilising every muscle and every faculty.

From the gastronomic as well as the therapeutic standpoint, the garden's speciality is the sixteenth and seventeenth century-style "sallet", mostly consisting of home-grown fruit, vegetable and herbs. The great herbalists (who were among the glories of the age of Shakespeare, Sidney, Bacon, Byrd, Milton, Marlowe, Hilliard, Herbert, Pepys, Purcell and

Newton) were fully aware of the value of wild and cultivated plants in building up as well as healing all the organs and faculties of the human system. A regular constituent of the diet of those days was a "sallet", comprising a far wider selection of ingredients than the standard salad of today. John Evelyn, the diarist and horticulturalist, lists more than eighty plants which regularly formed part of concoctions served at Tudor and Stuart tables[3]. Many of these plants are still prescribed by present-day herbalists and nutritionists as remedies for the same ills for which they were prescribed by their predecessors three or four centuries ago[4].

Most of them occur in my garden at Highwood Hill, where they are used as ingredients of the salads designed to build up the positive health of those who eat them. They also help to counteract atmospheric pollution and promote the health of their fellow plants by means of symbiotic processes. Herbs are regarded as sovereign links not only between plant but also between humanity and Gaia, helping to forge psychological roots in local ecosystems and to create niches for wildlife.

Forest gardens are being developed in several parts of Britain, including inner city areas, where they are spearheading a rural invasion of the townscape, reversing the predominant urban invasion of

3. *Acetaria, A Discourse of Sallets*, John Evelyn, 1699
4. See Appendix, page 152

the countryside. For example, one North London hillside is now covered with apple and apricot, peach and pear and other fruit trees, surrounded with red-, white- and blackcurrants and numerous aromatic herbs. Along with their accompanying birds and insects, these plants are bringing back beauty and fragrance to an urban landscape. A similar mix of plants combining nourishment with beauty has appeared in a new forest garden created on land belonging to the London Wildlife Trust. In a Birmingham inner city area, comprising a high proportion of people of Asian or Afro-Caribbean origin, a permaculture plot called Ashram Acres specialises in sub-tropical plants.

A forest garden is one example of a system of land-working, called agroforestry or permaculture, which has roots going back to humanity's earliest ages. It offers root-solutions to some of humanity's most urgent problems: those connected with environmental pollution and decline, hunger, disease, homelessness, and destitution. It is a system which imitates the multi-storey structure and diversity of the natural forest, in which every single plant has some useful function to perform. It offers a degree of productivity far in excess of any achieved by the most "advanced" systems of orthodox horticulture or agribusiness. Factory farming, far from being as intensively productive as claimed, uses vast acreages of cereals to feed the wretched inhabitants of veal crates and battery cages.

Oriental craftspeople are traditionally famed for their intricate workmanship and ingenuity. This enables them to excel in "hi-tech" industries, but is equally apparent in some of the gardens surrounding village homes. Many of these meticulously-designed gardens provide sophisticated, wholesome, and effective systems of satisfying human beings' basic needs — food, fibres, fuel, medicines and timber. These gardens, known as "homegardens" throughout the tropics, allow families to attain high degrees of self-sufficiency and economic security.

Among the best-known homegardens are the Kandyan forest gardens, averaging one hectare each, found in a hilly and densely populated area of central Sri Lanka. These gardens almost definitely originated two or three hundred years ago when Sri Lanka was famous as the "Land of Plenty and the Isle of Righteousness." This was a period of close and enlightened co-operation between the civil and Buddhist authorities, which led to the construction of an extensive network of irrigation canals and reservoirs, or "tanks".

An active attempt to restore this relationship between "temple and tank" is being made by the Sarvodaya Shramadana movement of agricultural and social regeneration. The main thrust of this movement, which is inspired not only by Buddhist teachings but also by Gandhi's Constructive Programme of worldwide renewal, is to restore the traditional self-reliance as well as the cultural and spiritual vitality of

24

the Sri Lankan village. The Sarvodaya philosophy is based on "the potential goodness of all human beings, their inalienable equality and the enormous heights to which human beings could rise if they only learn to help each other."

Most homegardens are found in areas where space is limited, such as islands or desert oases, or in regions of a population density several times higher than that of the industrialised West. In such regions people are not crowded together into vast, uniform council estates or tower blocks, but inhabit rural villages built of local materials and beautified by an abundance of varied vegetation. Their lives are stimulated and refreshed by the natural environment, and the labour-intensive work of the homegardens and their associated industries and crafts makes for full employment for all. Moreover, as almost all their needs are supplied by themselves or within their immediate bioregions (see Chapter 9), there is little atmospheric pollution from motor fumes or large factories or power-stations.

Co-operation, or mutual aid, is the keynote of the forest garden village system. But significant knowledge, or age-old wisdom, is also vitally important. Many villages seem to have inherited an encyclopaedic knowledge about the many different types of symbiotic relationships between different plants, and the way garden plants and practices can be manipulated, in order to maximise the beneficial effects of these relationships.

Agroforestry techniques can offer one practical solution for the reclamation of arid areas. China, Israel, Egypt are among those who have successfully restored desert areas to productivity. Deserts are estimated to cover one-third of the world's land-surface, and if more countries could reclaim these vast spaces this could provide room for millions of homeless and deprived people to build houses surrounded by homegardens, which would supply their basic needs and enable them to live fulfilled and happy lives.

One of the world's most enlightened countries is the small Central American state of Costa Rica. In a recent lecture about new crops, given at the Royal Botanic Gardens in London, the President of Costa Rica pledged that he would encourage his country to become a "pilot project of sustainable development." A conservation programme designed to create "an intelligent strategic balance with nature" would include a land-use plan allowing for 40 per cent of the country to be protected as national parks and reserves. It would also include a research project to catalogue the country's biodiversity – believed to constitute 5 per cent of the world's total, – and explore its expanded potential for satisfying human needs. A scheme was also proposed to encourage farmers to plant tree crops on land degraded by agriculture and to restore traditional farming techniques.

Costa Rica intends to participate in a joint project being assessed by Kew (the Royal Botanic Gardens) and Britain's Overseas Development Administration, to plant Inga trees as components of multi-purpose agroforestry schemes. Ingas are fast-growing nitrogen-fixing legumes with remarkable properties which make them suitable for restoring some of the many tropical rainforest areas which have been ruthlessly destroyed by logging and conversion to "hamburger ranches". Their properties include the ability to benefit other crop plants and to rehabilitate degraded acid soils by symbiotic processes. The trees, which are very beautiful, yield edible beans.

The Costa Rican initiative is one of many such examples which show that, despite actual or feared symptoms of environmental disaster and decline, Gaia's general state of health is fundamentally sound. "Miracles" are appearing on the horizon of ecological development and human well-being. In particular, implementation of agroforestry techniques could lead to healthy superproductivity on a level which has previously been thought impossible.

With our present knowledge, there is no technical reason why every woman, man and child on Gaia's Earth should not be adequately fed, clothed, housed, and given the opportunity for self-realisation. In the history of human evolution, a new species is appearing in many parts of the world – a species endowed with the mental, moral, and spiritual qualities fitting it to co-operate with Gaia's self-healing capacities. It would be positive to call the new species *Homo altruisticus*.

27

Chapter 1

Ourselves and Gaia

The unprecedented tribulations and traumas of this climactic period in world history can be seen as the birth-throes of a new age – the Age of Gaia.

Gaia was the name given by the ancient Greeks to the feminine attributes of the one God, as incarnated in Mother Earth. The scientist James Lovelock has demonstrated conclusively, through rigorous scientific reasoning, that the Earth is a unitary organism, with faculties, such as self-regulation and adaptation to environmental change, which are characteristic of biological entities such as the human system. Gaia is thus the supreme earthly manifestation of the yin processes in cosmic life.

Yin and yang are words coined by ancient Chinese philosophers to denote the basic feminine and masculine polarities. Yin is conservation, co-operation, compassion, caring, nurturing, integration, intuition, inspiration, beauty, harmony, ecology, rest, security, stability, and peace. It is also aspects of the dark side of life: fear, bondage, submissiveness, contraction, cruelty, docility, lethargy, and stagnation. Yang is will-power, creativity, individualism, inventiveness, adventurousness, pioneering, freedom, expansiveness, dynamic energy, courage, heroism, leadership, but also domination, greed, violence, antagonism, competition, destructiveness, exploitation, hate, fragmentation, scepticism, discord, and war.

The early Greek philosopher Heraclitus, who believed that the basic element in the universe was fire or radiation, affirmed that there was a fundamental pendulum tendency in all life, a swing between opposites, between discord and harmony, between challenge and response. He believed that true progress depended on wise manipulation of this process, in exactly the same way that drawing a bow with both hands causes the flight of an arrow, or plucking the strings of a lyre creates a musical note.

Evolution, or development, is a spiral process, combining an upward thrust with a horizontal swing between yin and yang. Although this process is continuous, there are also long periods when one tendency predominates, culminating in a critical turning-point when a violent swing of the pendulum

29

ushers in a period where the opposite will predominate. If you believe in reincarnation, you can easily imagine how a morally, emotionally, and spiritually progressive male could be re-born as a woman, and *vice versa*.

In the history of Western civilisation, such a critical turning-point occurred at the Renaissance. Then, the long yin period of the Dark Ages and Middle Ages, which followed the collapse of the Roman Empire, switched to an aggressively yang period which has continued to the present day. Today numerous indications suggest that we are in the throes of a similar mutationary shift. Certain yang forces have reached an intolerable pitch of greed, lust for power, savagery, and corruption, inflicting untold suffering on millions of human beings and other forms of life. This harshness causes an inevitable reaction in human consciousness, turning towards the gentle, constructive, nurturing processes associated with Mother Earth.

The early centuries of the first millennium AD saw the growth of the profoundly ecological and feminist creed of Celtic Christianity. In contrast to the intolerance of Rome towards "paganism" – the creed of the *pagani*, or peasants – the Celtic Christian missionaries grafted the Law of Love on to the best features of the old Nature-worship, combining the two creeds and converting the Mother Goddess Brigit (Bride) into a Christian saint. The great Irishman Columcille (Columba of Iona) seems to have practised the Law of Love to reconcile disputes between the four races inhabiting Scotland, reconciliation which led to the unified Scottish nation. Celtic Christianity was repressed by Rome, but its aesthetic and metaphysical beauties nonetheless made an irresistible impact on European culture.

The Arthurian legends embody, in symbolic form, many of the profoundest teachings of the Celtic saints. The Grail stories in particular depict the various stages of the yogic journey, or stages towards holistic development, which lies at the centre of all great religions. In these tales the revelation of the Grail chalice represents the stage of ecstatic enlightenment which is the peak experience, after the seeker has surmounted every challenge or ordeal which must be faced in order to gain spiritual experience and strength.

Europe was overwhelmingly rural through the Middle Ages, and the vast majority of its people were peasants, presumably with the virtues and faults of peasant and tribal societies throughout the world and throughout history: extreme conservatism, social cohesion, and closeness to the soil. Though the feudal system became widespread, difficulties of communications and harsh environments ensured that, very often, it was less oppressive than it was designed to be. The lord of a remote manor was far too dependent on his serfs and villeins for his very existence to dare to arouse their wrath and resistance by acts of cruelty and excessive demands.

The "cities" which grew up in the later mediaeval period would today be described as small market towns – centres for the distribution and processing of the products of the surrounding countryside, (or bioregion in today's language), to which they were inseparably linked. The great strength of many mediaeval cities lay in their free, co-operative craft-guilds, which enabled highly gifted men (or occasionally women) to develop their skills, unimpeded by oppressive market and feudal forces. The supreme artistic achievements of these guilds were the many cathedrals, at whose workmanship people still marvel today. Complementing cities' structures, monasteries were also centres of skill, culture and learning, and many were responsible for important developments of infrastructure such as draining marshes, reclaiming wastelands, and building bridges.

The dawning of the Renaissance led to dramatic changes. Since then, knowledge has continued to expand, causing the series of dramatic yang-events and yang-developments which have shaken Europe, America and the rest of the world ever since. A vast expansion of knowledge has been accompanied by colossal accumulations of wealth and power. These yang forces have combined to lead to degrees of destructiveness and environmental pollution which could lead to the extermination of all life on Earth.

After the horror of the bombing of Hiroshima, Einstein sent a telegram to members of the Emergency Committee of Atomic Scientists, of which he was President. It read: "Our world faces a crisis as yet unperceived by those possessing the power to make great decisions..... The unleashed power of the atom has changed everything save our ways of thinking, and thus we drift to an unparalleled catastrophe. A new way of thinking is essential if man is to survive and move toward higher levels." This 'new way of thinking' can be summed up in one word: *caring*. If only people *cared* about the fate of their neighbours. And in the modern world, caring about your neighbour means caring about yourself.

The developments of science and technology which started with Leonardo da Vinci and Galileo, led to Newton and the Industrial Revolution, to the harnessing of electricity and radiation, to flight and communications technology, as well as research into new-old methods of producing food and other basic necessities – all these open up incredibly positive prospects of a world order in which hunger, home-lessness, poverty, and even most disease could be a thing of the past.

Some of the latest discoveries of science confirm what religious leaders and philosophers have pro-claimed for thousands of years: we are all one. In the 1960s James Lovelock was asked by members of the staff of the Jet Propulsion Laboratories in California to devise some means of detecting evidence of life on Mars. After extensive research, aided by an American scientist, Dian Hitchcock, Lovelock decided that one approach to the solution of the problem would be to examine the Martian atmosphere. Analysing the chemical composition of the Earth's atmosphere, and taking into consideration the increasing amounts of solar radiation which have reached the Earth in the course of its history, Lovelock came to the astonishing conclusion that some means must exist for regulating the atmosphere, in order for Earth's ability to sustain life to be maintained. It was clear that no such devices existed on Mars, which meant that it was a dead planet.

Extending his research, Lovelock concluded that the Earth's regulating devices must form part of the biosphere – the sum-total of living beings that are the Earth's inhabitants. This led to the still more far-reaching hypothesis that "the entire range of living matter on Earth, from whales to viruses, and from oaks to algae, could be regarded as constituting a single living entity, capable of manipulating the Earth's atmosphere to suit its overall needs and endowed with faculties and powers far beyond those of its constituent parts."[1] For this entity the novelist William Golding suggested the name Gaia.

In this improbable way, the age-old concept of Mother Earth has received confirmation from the most advanced intellectual and technical resources of modern science. It is unlikely to be mere chance that the concept of the Earth Mother has been re-born in

1. *Gaia, A New Look at Life on Earth*, James Lovelock, Oxford University Press,1979

the consciousness of sophisticated Western men and women at this crucial turning-point in history.

Throughout history, at times of crises when yang forces have been causing widespread devastation and misery, human beings have turned in desperation to a compassionate female Deity – the Madonna in Europe, Kwanyin in China. Western science has now proved that such a Being really exists; that the natural environment is much more than an impersonal conglomeration of atoms, but is a feeling Presence, with whom we can relate, who suffers as we suffer, but who has immense stores of wisdom from which we can learn, wisdom derived from the Law of Love, which is the basic law of life.

Gaia is a Mother figure, progenitor of all living beings, who looks after us all and provides a rich environment that is capable of supplying the essential physical needs of all living beings, and many of our emotional and spiritual needs. She embodies precise laws and processes which, if conformed to, can lead to survival and self-fulfilment. Gaia is an evolving, purposive Being, who promotes and nurtures the evolution (development) of the multitude of other living beings that help to constitute her body. Such development is fundamentally different from the process known as "development" in political and economic circles today, which involves deceit, disillusion, and disappointment for millions, who find their hopes of material affluence converted into poverty, misery, and debt-slavery.

But the fact that Earth has been proved to be a super-organism does not mean that Gaia is an infallible and invulnerable goddess. On the contrary, she has sustained innumerable terrible wounds, especially since the start of World War Two. The survival of life depends upon healing those wounds and reversing the forces and processes that created them.

Practical material steps have been well publicised by the Green movement. The most effective comprehensive, constructive answer to the problem must be to conserve existing trees while launching a huge worldwide programme of tree-planting. Trees absorb carbon dioxide, the main "greenhouse" gas, as well as industrial pollutants, while exhaling oxygen, which is a basic necessity for all forms of life. Trees also create rain by transpiring water into the atmosphere through their leaves, and control the groundwater system through their roots; in this way they help to prevent both droughts and floods. They also temper the climate, reduce the destructive power of winds, and provide shade and shelter for other forms of life. As well as all this, they supply food, timber, fuel, energy, fibres, and other human necessities.

I have spent much of my life planting trees and encouraging others to do so, to preserve and conserve our precious but much-abused planet. One of my current projects involves the restoration of a patch of land back to its original forest state. If we give something vital back to the Earth, she will be able to treat us well.

Other practical steps to healing Gaia include reducing consumption of fossil fuels, eliminating emissions of nuclear and other toxic wastes, and composting organic wastes, such as sewage and garbage, so that they can be returned to the land. Lovelock hints that biological, psychological, and even religious factors are also involved: "Modern medicine recognises the mind and body as part of a single system, where the state of each can affect the health of the other. It may be true also in planetary medicine that our collective attitude towards the Earth affects and is affected by the health of the planet. Christian teaching has it that the body is the temple of the soul, and that this alone is a good enough reason for leading a healthy life. I find myself looking on the Earth itself as a place for worship, with all life as its congregation. For me this is reason enough for doing everything that is in my power to sustain a healthy planet."[2]

If Gaia is indeed an intelligent, purposeful and biological entity, with faculties and organs similar to our own, then one of her outstanding features must be her cohesiveness, the precise co-ordination of all her parts and activities. This basic characteristic of life (any textbook on physiology gives innumerable examples) confirms Kropotkin's conviction that mutual aid, rather than competition, provides the principal dynamic force in evolution.

2. *Gaia: The Practical Science of Planetary Medicine*, James Lovelock, Gaia Books, London, 1991

Jungian psychology also makes clear that evolution –
holistic development – should be the central feature
of the healing process, whether mental, physical,
emotional, or spiritual. To be effective, healing must
go beyond the restoration of a pre-existent state of
relative harmony. It should lead to a higher level of
all-round development, and should thus involve the
whole system. Disease can be transcended and
transmuted into an agent of progress by the counter-
forces that it arouses. Jung's psychology additionally
maintains that the psyche contains layers of subliminal awareness, linking every individual to the family
and other communal organisms to which it belongs,
including the natural world – Gaia. The part cannot
be separated from the whole.

Holistic therapy confirms this thesis. It maintains
that the individual organ must be treated in the context of the entire system and environment; that it is
affected by the state of the whole, and in its turn,
affects the whole. All living beings, including ourselves, are parts of Gaia. All forms of life are both
inseparable from and interrelated to each other.
However small and insignificant an individual entity
may seem, its health is influenced by – and influences
– the health of Gaia herself. As Gaia is an evolving
entity, there must be a pattern, a blueprint, a design
for growth in every one of her constituent parts, just
as there is a DNA helix in every cell of our own
bodies. Our own holistic development cannot be
separated from the evolution of Gaia herself.

Holistic development also involves us recognising and acting upon our latent potentialities for health in body, mind, soul, and spirit. These potentialities are the four walls of any house of health. Goethe maintained that a living organism is characterised by the fact that "the whole is more than the sum of its parts." Spirit is the "fourth dimension" that integrates and empowers the three "human dimensions" – physical, mental and emotional.

In order to live in harmony with Gaia, and thus with ourselves and others, we must take full responsibility for ourselves. Many of us come up against a great number of physical, mental and emotional onslaughts during our lives. The best way to counter these pressures is through trying to resist them with mantramistic declarations of Truth. In this way we eventually learn how to transmute problems into strength and wisdom.

The human body, like other living organisms, is a marvellously intricate, minutely co-ordinated and efficiently regulated system. It possesses innumerable devices within its immune system for warding off the attacks of germs and toxins and counteracting their ill-effects. Natural healing and health-building is primarily concerned with understanding the health-giving processes in our bodies, and finding means of supporting and facilitating them. We all have a positive duty to care for ourselves rather than relying for care on unnatural drug therapies which supplant and suppress our natural physical processes.

Chapter 2

The Role of Plants

Some of the most obvious links between ourselves and Gaia are immediately apparent when we look at the role of plants in our lives. Plants, highly complex living organisms, are among the most potent of Gaia's agents for working out her constructive and compassionate aims. The influence of plants on our lives is overwhelmingly beneficial.

The majority of the foods and liquids we consume and the medicines we swallow are either plants or of plant origins. It has become rather a cliché to state "we are what we eat", but this does not make it any less true. We should never forget that our bodies are made of the foods, liquids and medicines that we consume, the air that we breathe and the thoughts that we think. This means that, to a far greater extent than most of us realise, we can take command over our own health. The human system, which is an enormously complicated organism, requires a wide diversity of plant foods to supply the numerous proteins, carbohydrates, vitamins, minerals, enzymes and other nutrients necessary for the positive, radiant and vibrant health that should be the heritage of every human being.

Gaia is prodigal in the profusion and diversity of plants which she makes available for the satisfaction of most human needs, physical as well as aesthetic, emotional, and spiritual needs. Yet the full potential of plant life is largely ignored in most cultures today. Instead, much of the land is given over to monocropping. Vast acreages of healthy forest are ruthlessly destroyed for the sake of one single product – timber – or in order to be replaced by pastures growing one single species – grass – to be cropped by one type of animal – beef cattle. Such insane improvidence is completely unsustainable. It will inevitably lead to wholesale starvation among wide sections of the world's rapidly increasing population, unless we act unilaterally to reverse the trend.

Human genius is quite incapable of reproducing the mysterious process of photosynthesis. In this process the green pigment in plants, chlorophyll, combines carbon dioxide from the atmosphere with water and minerals from the soil, and uses the sun's energy to create carbohydrates. This is the basis of all physical life. The chemical composition of chlorophyll is similar to human blood, and a pure bloodstream is the essence of health. Leading nutri-·tionists, such as Bircher-Benner (the inventor of muesli), have long maintained that our diet should always contain a large proportion of pure, fresh, raw, organically grown green leaves to ensure that we maintain a pure and healthy bloodstream.

Second in importance for positive health are fruit sugars, which are powerful brain foods and essential for high levels of energy. It seems that grapes, like green foods, have a special affinity for the blood. Perhaps Jesus realised that when he equated wine with blood at the Last Supper? Taking a periodic grape cure has been an established practice in Europe for centuries, particularly in the vineyards of Germany, and the benefits are well recognised: cleansing the blood and revitalising the entire system. Grape cures have even reportedly helped heal supposedly "incurable" diseases – a South African doctor, Johanna Brandt,[1] has described how an exclusive diet of grapes cured her of an advanced case of cancer.

After experimentation, and following extensive documented nutritional research, I have found my ideal diet for optimum positive health. I call it the

1. *The Grape Cure*, Basil Shackleton, Thorsons, Wellingborough, UK. 1979

R70 diet. This consists of at least 70 per cent raw, unprocessed, organically grown, fresh or sun-dried fruit, vegetables, cereals, nuts, herbs, spices, and cold-pressed vegetable oils. The remaining 30 per cent can include wholemeal bread or biscuits, lightly cooked or steamed vegetables, pure unchemicalised yeast or soya flavourings (such as tofu mayonnaise or miso) and one hundred per cent fruit jams. Sugar is totally excluded and salt largely avoided.

Gluten is the gluey protein of wheat, oats, barley and rye, and it tends to clog the system and inhibit free circulation of blood, lymph, and other bodily fluids essential for maximum energy and vitality. Therefore gluten cereals should only be eaten in moderation, but you can replace them with rice, millet, maize, buckwheat, and pulses, which are at least as palatable. So-called primitive cultures – which usually had few dietary problems – used a variety of plant flours from seeds and trees. Few of these flours are currently commercially available, but you can forage for your own – with the aid of a good guide. In a future Age of Agroforestry tree cereals such as chestnut and mesquite flours will undoubtedly be used widely once again.

This sort of diet not only promotes individual health, but is very resource-efficient, and can be produced in most areas of the world – with obvious positive implications for healthy global economics.

It is best to avoid all animal products as they tend to clog the system and provoke acid reactions. In the

Far East soya products are common substitutes for milk and cheese, as is nutritious coconut cream, made of crushed coconut meat, which is an essential ingredient of much of South East Asian cookery.

All salads should include raw or dried herbs, which add interest and increase nutritional value. Numerous excellent herbals spanning many centuries have documented the ways that specific herbs have special affinities for the body's most vital organs, such as the heart, brain, eyes, liver, nerves and glands. For thousands of years they have been used for healing diseases. Some whole raw herbs can do better than heal – they can prevent disease by building up all-round health and immunity

We have grown out of the habit of using wild plants as ingredients, but "weeds" including nettles, dandelions, and sorrel, as well as wild berries such as rowan berries, are full of valuable minerals and other nutrients. Many plants that have come to be seen as weeds were introduced into our gardens centuries ago as food, so don't ignore them. They can add interesting seasonal variety to your food, as well as nutrients, but if you find they taste rather harsh cook them lightly or marinade them with dressings.

It is never a good idea to make drastic changes to change your diet in a hurry, so if you decide to move towards a R70 diet it could take some time to accomplish. But the change should be found entirely worthwhile in terms of health, energy, clearheadedness, and zest for living. You are also sure to come to find the fresh, natural aromatic flavours of foods straight from soil, bush, or tree more enjoyable than the junk foods that fill supermarket shelves, or even haute cuisine! But don't rush the change, you must feel right about making it.

As this type of eating becomes more and more prevalent – as it must for the healthy survival of ourselves and our planet, the importance of our plant heritage will become increasingly apparent. In the West we use remarkably few of our natural plant resources, relying instead on the few crops produced in subsidised monocultures, while some other countries still value and use their local plant life. The inhabitants of Java, for example, consume more than 500 different plant foods. There is beginning to be a vital resurgence of interest in saving seeds and looking at local plant diversity and natural ecology. Let's hope that this interest has come in time to stop the disastrous trend of the past fifty years toward ever increasing genetic similarity.

Two men who unveiled something of the almost infinite potential in plant life were Luther Burbank, probably the most famous name in plant breeding, and George Washington Carver, inventor of peanut butter and many other products derived from the humble peanut, as well as from soya beans and sweet potatoes. Both were devoutly religious men; they did not research using sophisticated technology, but relied instead on prayer, inspiration, and telepathic communication with plants for their hugely successful achievements. "The secret of improved plant breeding, apart from scientific knowledge, is love," Burbank told Paramahansa Yogananda. "While I was conducting experiments to make 'spineless' cacti, I often talked to the plants to create a vibration of love. 'You have nothing to fear,' I would tell them. 'You don't need your defensive thorns. I will protect you.' Gradually the useful plant of the desert emerged in a thornless variety."[2]

Manley P. Hall, a Californian philosopher, asserted that Burbank's "power of love" was a subtle kind of nourishment that made everything grow better. Burbank explained that in his experiments he took plants into his confidence, asked them to help, and assured them that he respected their small lives and regaded them with deep affection. In a lecture to the American Pomological Society titled *How to Produce New Fruits and Flowers*[3], he said: "Preconceived notions, dogmas and all personal prejudice and bias must be laid aside. Listen patiently, quietly and reverently to the lessons, one by one, which Mother Nature has to teach, shedding light on that which was before a mystery, so that all who will, may see and know. She conveys her truths only to those who are passive and receptive. Accepting these truths as suggested, wherever they may lead, then we have the

2. *The Secret Life of Plants*, Tompkins and Bird, Penguin Books, London, 1975
3, *ibid*

whole universe in harmony with us. At last man has found a solid foundation for science, having discovered that he is part of a universe which is eternally unstable in form, eternally immutable in substance."

Over 1,000 new varieties of fruits, vegetables and flowers provide plenty of practical proof of the effectiveness of Burbank's beliefs and methods of working. Many of these varieties are still available in the United States through seed catalogues.

A similar combination of mysticism with intimate observation of nature and endless practical experimentation characterised the work of George Washington Carver. Inspired by a desire to help poor cotton farmers in the southern states of America, most of whom were black like himself, Carver spent ten years studying the soils which had become degraded through monocropping. Eventually he decided that the answer lay in the peanut, then a largely neglected crop, which could both grow in poor soils and inject them with nitrogen. Carver also discovered that the peanut had vast potential for human benefit, not only as a food, but also as a source of protein-rich oil.

As a result of his research, the peanut became a major crop throughout the southern states. Carver was elected a fellow of the Royal Society and two of the leading industrialists of his time, Ford and Edison, offered to employ him at large salaries. But Carver believed that his discoveries should be made available to suffering humanity free of charge. "God did not charge you or me for making peanuts," he said. "Why should I profit from their products?" When pressed to explain the reasons for his fantastic success, Carver gave the simple answer, "The secrets are in the plants. To elicit them you have to love them enough."[4]

Another devout researcher into the mysteries of plant life was the Austrian herbalist Maria Treben. Her principal aim was to help people suffering from the "diseases of civilisation" by re-introducing them to the simple plant remedies used by their ancestors. A profound believer in self-healing, she wrote: "To find a way out of the hopelessness of ill health by one's own strength and free will is, thanks to nature's medicinal herbs, humanly elevating. To win back one's health, and to bear responsibility for oneself, elevates human dignity to such a degree that the sick person is taken halfway to recovery from the hopelessness of his sick life."[5]

As a young girl, while staying with a forest-ranger, Maria Treben studied wild plants and gained intuitive insights into the interrelationships of nature. She also believed that she was inspired by the Virgin Mary. Personal experience reinforced her great faith in herbal remedies. Shortly after her marriage she became ill with typhoid fever, caused by contaminated meat.

....

4. *The Secret Life of Plants, op cit*
5. *Health from God's Pharmacy*, Maria Treben, Ennsthaler, Austria, 1984

She spent more than six months in hospital, but the after-effects of typhoid persisted after she returned home. One day a woman brought her a bottle of a herbal formula called Swedish Bitters (concocted in 1850 by the Swedish doctor, Dr Samst, who died as a result of a riding accident aged 103). After she had applied the bitters as a compress to her abdomen, it seems that all her typhoid symptoms disappeared, never to return. Maria Treben had many experiences of the remarkable effectiveness of various herbal remedies, both in her own case and for the many sufferers who consulted her.

Traditional herbal doctors, going right back to Paracelsus and the earliest known physicians, have always known that the body needs a regular intake of bitter herbs. They stimulate the eliminative functions of the liver and counteract the cloying effects of fats, allowing the digestion to work efficiently.

I have found that one of the great benefits of the R70 diet has been to revive my basic nutritional instinct. In our society eating can provoke all sorts of anxieties, but when this instinct, this body-awareness that we share with animals, is fully aroused, the anxiety is taken out of eating and drinking. I have come to know intuitively when and what to eat and drink and when and what not to. If illness threatens, I am able to act with the natural wisdom given by Gaia to all her creatures, and I adopt a simple regime of resting and fasting, apart from a few curative herbs eaten whole or taken as tea. This regime allows the body to mobilise all its forces and its age-old inherited ingenuity to expel all invading toxins.

Another very important reason for eating a good proportion of raw fruit, vegetables, and wholemeal cereals is to consume the fibre, or roughage, which improves digestion and elimination. The fibres in foods are parts of plants that play key roles in their structure, metabolism, and self-healing processes. They include polysaccharides and lignin which support the firmness of cell walls and gums and mucilages which repair injured tissues. Eating sufficient fibre keeps your insides clean, helping to remove toxins and even heavy metals from your system. Some raw plant foods can tend to taste harsh or bitter, a taste developed by the plants in their efforts to sustain their struggles for existence. I like to think that ingesting these foods helps to build up my own 'moral fibre' – stamina and endurance!

Traditional societies have always known about plants' qualities. Our sceptical society today is continuously proving the reasons for plants' successes with scientific explanations as well as through historical research. Leslie and Susannah Kenton, a mother-and-daughter team who have written about eating raw food[6], state: "We find, as others have, that the harder we work the greater the percentage of raw food we need to eat in order to function at top peak

6. *Raw Energy*, Susannah and Leslie Kenton, Century, London, 1984

mentally and physically.... When we changed to a high-raw diet, we found we could write and research efficiently for much longer periods.... We also needed less sleep. And when we did sleep, our sleep was deeper and more restful."

The essence of all-round positive health, vitality and energy in any biological organism comes from unimpeded circulation of the blood and other bodily fluids. Without free circulation, blockages occur, the blood becomes clogged with impurities, energy becomes locked up and poisonous substances accumulate, leading to inevitable disease. Many symptoms of disease, such as coughing, rashes, and fever, represent a healing crisis. This is when the body makes a concentrated effort to rid itself of toxins by every means in its power. Symptoms can appear alarming, but a knowledgeable healer will usually interpret them as the body at work. One of the main purposes of natural remedies is to support the bodily organs in their own co-ordinated efforts to free themselves of toxic burdens.

The essential oils of aromatic plants are among the many tools employed by Gaia's agents in the plant world to help humans and animals in their struggles against disease and pests. The biological purpose of plant scents is to attract beneficial insects and other organisms, and to deter and drive out harmful ones. Many plant scents have remarkable penetrating powers. They can travel up the nose and enter the limbic system in the brain. From there they can proceed to the areas of the brain which control heart-beat, blood pressure, breathing and the emotions. The limbic system is also connected with the glands and nerves, and these can convey the fragrances to many parts of the body. Thus, almost the entire human system and its constituent organs can be steeped in plant essences, stimulating the flow of energy and driving out impurities. Plants not only support and heal us through physical nourishment, they can also nourish our emotions and our spirit.

Aromatherapy is a new-old science concerned with the remarkable purifying and healing power of plant odours. Studied by the ancient Egyptians, Greeks, and Romans, it was revived early this century by the French chemist René-Maurice Gattefosse. Fragrant plants often have specific healing properties, and have an important part to play in combatting industrial pollution. All gardeners should plant aromatic trees, bushes, flowers, and herbs to purify the atmosphere, particularly in built-up areas. Simply working in a scented garden can be a calming and stimulating "aromatherapy treatment" in itself.

Gaia's plants, with their intriguing scents, colours, and forms perform valuable functions in promoting human emotional and even spiritual development. When we approach the miracles of Nature with love and humility we become open to enjoy her healing and regenerating powers.

"Earth is, not only the mother of the young, the strong, the magnificent, whose tired muscles and long-limbed grace are the embodiment of her physical life, in whose eager glance burns the vitality of her spirit; she is also the pitiful mother of those who have lost all.... The spirit that was so desolate, lost in the strange atmosphere of physical inferiority, may once more feel the zest that he thought was gone for ever. And this zest is health: sweeping into the mind and into those recesses of mind beyond the conscious self, it overflows into the body. Very often this great rush of joy... brings back perfect health. Even in diseases that are at present called incurable, that are purely physical, no one will deny the alleviation resulting from this new life. It is possible that, as spiritual ties between man and nature grow stronger, all disease may vanish before the vitality that will stream into us so swiftly, so easily, because it will not be confined to one channel."[7]

7. *The Spring of Joy*, Mary Webb, Cape, London, 1928

Chapter 3

Mind and the Life-Force

Throughout my life, from early childhood, I have been striving to deal with my own and my family's health problems by non-chemical means, and have researched continuously into natural and spiritual methods of healing and health-building. I have learnt enough, and had sufficient success, to know that I am working on the right lines.

One of the essential factors in building up positive health and strength is consistent positive thinking. You can only achieve this by setting a clear goal or series of goals, and having the determination to attain these goals at all costs. This has the effect of focussing, concentrating, and unifying all your forces and faculties. Antagonism, far from weakening your resolve, can strengthen and vitalise it by the adrenalin it arouses. Stress, which is widely recognised by the medical profession as one of the major causes of the diseases of civilisation, is the result of negative thinking. Consistent positive thinking, in contrast, inevitably leads to physical control and development of 'kinaesthetic awareness', or body-consciousness. You can derive enormous physical and mental benefits when you learn to perform every action in a controlled, rhythmic way, consciously exercising every muscle involved.

The most valuable exercise is the performance of useful tasks in a strong, purposeful way combined with meditation, so that your mind is in tune with your body. The best of all forms of exercise for me is PMG – Purposeful Meditative Gardening. When gardening, all your activities, mental and physical, are vitalised by fresh, fragrant air and a beautiful stimulating environment in direct contact with Gaian influences. In gardening you use every muscle, and, if you are growing wholesome food and herbs to benefit yourself, your family, and others, your work is dignified by the thought that you are satisfying basic human needs. Purposeful Meditative Gardening is working together with nature, with Gaia, to fulfil her design, while finding roots – as much as any of the plants – in the stability and security of her soil.

The calm, constructive, rhythmic work of gardening is highly conducive to meditation; it helps me to think positively and creatively about every topic that comes to mind, from trivial personal concerns to world problems. I find that strenuous, rhythmical exercise is conducive to powerful, positive thinking. It can even lead to very powerful insights.

We all have different ways of gaining insights, of reaching personal goals, and overcoming personal difficulties. In order even to start the journey towards fulfilment we must be open and receptive to positive influences, wherever they spring from. One of the greatest names in natural healing today is Meir Schneider. Born blind in the Ukraine, he emigrated with his family to Israel, and, having healed himself of blindness to the extent that he now has a driving licence, he is today director of the Center and School for Self-Healing, San Francisco.

The strongest influences on his early life were those of two exceptionally loving women: his grandmother Savta and Miriam, the owner of a library in Tel Aviv, who first introduced him to the techniques of bodywork. Schneider has gone on to develop and refine these techniques, and they have chiefly been responsible for remarkable achievements in healing himself and thousands of others, many of whom were branded by the medical profession as "incurable". Behind his bodywork are powerful mental, spiritual, and emotional resources: an indomitable will and extreme sensitivity combined with an enormous love for humanity which he believes he inherited as a child from his grandmother.

Schneider affirms that the individual mind is in constant dialogue with the "world mind", the mind of Gaia. "Any individual act reverberates through the world mind for all of humanity." He writes: "The mind is a non-material awareness which inhabits every part of the body.... For any change to take place in the body, it must first be accepted by the mind. It is not possible to heal the body without engaging the mind's support...Understanding that the mind governs the body is the first vital step towards understanding the body and its functions. The mind uses the body to translate thought into physical reality."[1]

Some cultures have always viewed holistic healing as the natural way. The connection between bodily movement, the mind, psychic force, and nature, is central to Traditional Chinese Medicine (TCM), which is now gaining increasing credence in the West. The Chinese believe in a psychic force, or life-force, called *qi*. They maintain that it is ever-present throughout the world – throughout Gaia – and within the human body, in which it flows through channels called meridians. Though neither *qi* nor the meridians are recognised in orthodox Western anatomy and physiology, the control of *qi* by acupuncture and the process called *qi-gong* brings real and undeniable material benefits. Acupuncture, for example, is commonly used by Chinese surgeons –

1.*Self-Healing: My Life and Vision*, Meir Schneider, Arkana, London, 1989

57

and increasingly in the West – as a substitute for anaesthetics when performing surgical operations. It has proved extremely successful in suppressing pain. *Qi-gong* is the control of *qi* by the mind or will for healing and health-building.

Hundreds of thousands of Chinese practise *T'ai chi-chuan* every day, out of doors and in all weathers. They consider that these rhythmic exercises cause *qi* to circulate freely in their bodies, thus balancing the yang and yin processes and promoting health. *T'ai chi* forms part of the system of natural living which has been regarded as an essential feature of the Chinese way of life since time immemorial. The ancient religion-philosophy of Taoism, a dominant influence in Chinese life for millennia, is based on the concept of Tao, which has been translated as 'The Way'. The basic scripture of Taoism is the *Tao të Ching*, which describes the Tao as "the Mother of all things". It says, "All-pervading is the Great Tao.... All things depend on it for life, and it rejects them not. It loves and nourishes all things."

Chinese philosophy celebrates the unity between mind, body, and the world. But Newtonian physics, which has dominated Western medical thinking since the seventeenth century, discounts any real possibilities of mutual influence between mind and body. However, as we move towards the new millenium there is a growth of New Physics, a view of science which has been developing since Quantum Theory was put forward in the early years of the twentieth century. New Physics seems to incorporate a slight trend towards a more holistic view of the world, and the obliteratation of hard-and-fast distinctions between mind and matter. There is also an increasing interest in anthroposophical science, based on the work of Rudolf Steiner, strongly influenced by Goethe. Central to this science is the assumption that matter does not exist objectively, but the human relationship is vital to any definition. This means that an object can only be defined when the human observer's perceptions of that object are included in that definition.

As a result of dissatisfaction with conventional medical practices, there are now signs that even the healing professions in the West may be moving towards a more holistic attitude, the idea that all life is one. The latter part of the twentieth century has seen the rise of a plethora of alternative therapies, and most people are now aware that it is possible to gain health in ways other than the rigidly conventional channels. The best health practitioners realise that healing involves not only the individual body, mind, soul, and spirit, but also their relation to the communal, cultural, and natural environment, and to humanity as a whole.

When you are aware of the world around you, you begin to notice some of the extraordinary forces which are constantly at work in Gaia's realm. More and more attention is being paid to the magnetic fields which appear to surround all living organisms, including plants. F.S.C. Northrop[2] and other leading scientists have suggested that these fields might contain the "structural information" which regulates the growth and unique characteristics of the individual organism. This also brings the modern scientist close to one of the fundamental convictions of ancient religious thinkers and philosophers: that a plane of consciousness called Truth or Reality exists where perfect "ideas" or "forms" of all phenomena can be found, together with designs or blueprints for their potential development.

Permanent union with this state of consciousness constitutes the enlightenment which is the ultimate aim of the yogic quest. Any individual, whatever his or her state of development, can have temporary access to it by constructing a precise mental picture of the organ or condition which needs to be healed in its perfect state. With practice this process, usually called visualisation, can be an incredibly strong healing force. The mind can become capable of precisely controlling *qi* which is the force mainly responsible for healing and growth. Anybody can become practised at using this entirely natural practice: for example, if you have a headache, try and visualise the headache itself; then visualise the headache disappearing, leaving health and comfort, simply and effectively. Visualisation has even been used as therapy for patients with advanced cancer, where the

2. *Raw Energy*, Leslie and Susannah Kenton, Century, 1984

patients are instructed to try and visualise healthy cells actually eating up the cancer cells. There have been some astonishing results. This visualisation process brings about an increasing clarity of consciousness, a "prayer of affirmation" which is a potent source of inner strength and will power.

One way toward natural holistic health, practised for many centuries, is yoga. There are many different streams of yoga, one that I have found particularly helpful is Raja Yoga. The Sanskrit term used for the higher plane of consciousness reached as a result of a successful struggle against antagonistic, manipulative forces is *Virya*. The aim of Raja Yoga is to reach *Virya*, defined as "energy, determination, courage, all aspects of an indomitable will which overcomes all obstacles and forces its way to the desired goal."

A commentary by Prof I.K. Taimni on the Yoga Sutras of Patanjali[3], one of the principal textbooks of Raja Yoga, states: "Great intensity of desire polarises all the mental faculties and powers and thus helps very greatly the realisation of one's aims." We can all aim for, and even reach, such intense and positive ways of thinking and being. Meir Schneider certainly showed this "great intensity of desire" in his battle against blindness. It was without doubt an important factor in his amazing success.

Positive health is not a mere absence of illness but all-round self-fulfilment, self-realisation, the realisa-

3. *The Science of Yoga*, T.P.H.Wheaton, Illinois, USA, 1981

tion of one's true, unique, God-given identity. It is a vitalised, co-ordinated functioning of the whole system – mental, emotional, and spiritual as well as physical. It involves a concentrated and continuous drive to understand and release your true selfhood, to bring out your latent potentialities, to find your true vocation, to discover the sources of your mental and physical energy and the secrets of constructive self-adaptation to circumstances.

The period since the Industrial Revolution has seen a long chain of technological "miracles". These achievements have one factor in common: precise obedience to the physical laws involved. Equal "miracles" are possible in the fields of health, wholeness and longevity, if we show equal obedience to the laws of life, respecting Gaia. Health-building or holistic development is an all-round continuous process. We should follow a life-style based on the laws of health rather than on the symptoms and causes of disease. Unlike Western orthodox medicine, Chinese systems of health have always recognised these laws: the aim of a Chinese doctor is to build up and maintain positive health, rather than postponing action until a patient becomes ill.

Every way we interact with our environment affects our wellbeing. We all want freedom, and the primary elements of freedom can be found in our own minds. As Milton wrote in *Paradise Lost*: "The mind is its own place, and can make a heaven of hell, a hell of heaven." Freedom is not just absence of external oppression or bondage, but a state of wholeness which exists at the very centre of our being, and which we should all cultivate. This can involve every detail of our lives, in a conscious and constantly exhilarating attempt to live creatively.

At times of crisis, danger, turmoil, and uncertainty throughout history, human beings have sought spiritual strength, security, and stillness in the concept of the Absolute. This concept seems to exist deep in the unconsciousness of all of us, and its symbol is the circle. When combined with a four-sided figure such as a square or cross, the symbol becomes a mandāla, which seems to denote the relative, earthly life, under the protection of the Absolute. The two symbols of circle and mandāla crop up in unexpected places, from palaeolithic sunwheel markings on rocks in Zimbabwe to the dreams and spontaneous drawings of psychiatric patients. They obviously represent a very deep-seated yearning of the human soul for certainty, for wholeness, for a fixed point in the midst of chaos.

Circles with obvious religious and/or defensive significance are found in the landscapes of many parts of the world. These may appear as standing-stones, or as the banks and ditches of Iron Age hill-forts. In recent decades, air photography has revealed circular markings in soil and crops of many parts of Britain. Many of these may indicate the sites of Celtic Christian monasteries – rings of family huts surrounding a central chapel – or stockaded villages.

Some have been interpreted as cattle corrals. One mystery of recent years has been the appearance of crop circles in cornfields in Britain. These shapes in the corn are usually complex and resemble some ancient religious or mystical symbol. Although some people dismiss them as elaborate hoaxes, they hold a much deeper potential significance for others.

In religious art, sanctity is denoted by the halo or aureole of light surrounding the head or body of a saintly figure. This is taken as an indication that the person has attained enlightenment at the climax of the yogic quest – a state involving unity with the Absolute and immortality. But the circle may also denote the beginning as well as the end of the quest: the seed of perfection implanted by God in the soul of each one of us, the innate Truth of our Beings.

Holistic development involves us in discovering, nurturing, and fostering the growth of this seed. This process is sometimes symbolised by mandālas in the form of flowers, which are rooted in the dark soil of the unconscious. A mandāla may also be interpreted as a representation of the fertilised ovum or the cell with its indwelling DNA, waiting to develop into a biological organism. We are made from millions of such cells, destined to adopt highly individual forms, designed to perform highly individual functions: nerve cells, blood cells, gland cells, muscle cells, skin cells. In a healthy body, all these organs are perfectly integrated with each other, with all their operations perfectly co-ordinated.

These organs, like sub-atomic particles studied by post-Newtonian physicists, can only be fully understood when their relationship to other organs and particles is taken into consideration. The human body is a complex, closely co-ordinated and finely regulated co-operative system, in which "the whole is more than the sum of its parts". This whole-making power, undetectable by the instruments of orthodox physics, is *qi*. This power is one of the most striking examples of the principle of cohesion, of mutual aid – of love – which is the basic law of life.

The complexity of the human body is more than reflected in the complexity of mind. For me, one of the most influential thinkers of this century is Carl Gustave Jung. According to Jung, the psyche comprises many levels, like the "storeys" of the forest. The ordinary person is normally unaware of most of these levels, as they are concealed within the unconscious. By way of the collective unconscious, we are all linked to far reaches of the Earth and the past, to our ancestors, to strange races, even to animals and plants. We are ultimately linked to Gaia herself.

Within the unconscious of each one of us are undreamt-of potentialities waiting to be discerned and developed – artistic creativity and scientific inventiveness, sensitivity, joy and suffering, the power to bestow happiness and the ability to inflict pain. Jung called the key organs of the unconscious *archetypes*, corresponding to the principal organs of the body. These are inherited patterns of behaviour, potential talents, and intellectual and emotional resources, often represented in dreams by mythical figures, such as Artemis and Aphrodite, Herakles and Odysseus. Without realising it, these archetypes constantly influence our thoughts and lives, arousing exalted ideals, disturbing presentiments, powerful urges, unacknowledged tensions and fears.

Traditional philosophers have claimed that the human being is a microcosm and the whole history of the Earth is constantly being re-enacted in the depths of the human psyche. So it is unsurprising that individuals and whole societies are constantly committing irrational and damaging acts. Yet we are *not* helpless victims of unconscious forces. If we use the power of our minds in a positive way we can overcome even major problems. Every individual can discover the technique of transmutation, and transform negative pressures (internalised or external) into spiritual strength and experience.

No-one should suggest that this is an easy process, but we can fearlessly face up to challenges. We can refuse to give in. Adrenalin activated by the challenges themselves can push us towards the clarity of mind and stamina which will allow us to find the right ways forward. But we never have to depend on ourselves alone. As all religions make clear, there are powers, agents of the One Supreme Power, that can be called upon for aid and guidance, if we try and live our lives according to Her/His laws.

Chapter 4

Foods of the Soul

To be healthy is to nurture our bodies, our minds, and our souls. We must begin our journey to health by eating a careful balanced diet, by taking exercise, and by appreciating the natural world around us. But we should also be aware of other dimensions.

Try and make time in your life for literature, music, and art. These soul foods can both inspire and inform us, yet they are too often relegated to a secondary place in many people's busy schedules. The arts also show us aspects of the universality of the world mind. They have given me great reserves of strength and helped me to gain some powerful insights at both difficult and joyous times of my life.

The tensions, power, and passion, the gaiety, violence, and suffering portrayed in Shakespeare's plays came out of deep emotions and urges at a crucial turning-point in world history. The plays are supreme poetry rather than the dry prose of the historian, philosopher, or legislator. Therefore they can speak to the immortal soul of humanity that is as alive today as when the plays were written. Their messages and the solutions they offer are just as valid today. Although they describe ways of life, customs and environments very different from ours, the soul-qualities, which contain the basic causative factors in all human problems, are universal.

Perhaps Shakespeare's key drama, in terms of historical, transitional forces, is King Lear. The king symbolises the dying feudal system, Edmund the bastard the emerging capitalist class, and Cordelia the feminist principles of humanity, compassion and integrity characteristic of the Age of Gaia, whose reign is yet to come. It has been proposed that Cordelia represents nature in the sense in which the Elizabethans understood her. Nature was then perceived as an ordered and beautiful arrangement, an outside force which showed individuals the appropriate ways of performing their duties.

"The idea of Nature, then, in orthodox Elizabethan thought, is always something normative for human beings. It is impossible to talk about Nature without talking also about pattern and ideal form; about Reason as displayed in Nature; about

Law as the innermost expression of Nature; about Custom which is the basis of Law and equally with Law an expression of Nature's pattern; about Restraint as the observance of Law, and the way to discover our richest self-fulfilment."[1]

From the little that is known about Shakespeare's life and from the internal evidence of the plays and poems, it seems clear that he was deeply and sometimes dangerously involved with a group of brilliant and cultured but corrupt and unstable members of the nobility, known as the Wilton Group. Their main activity was political intrigue, and Shakespeare's plays were used as propaganda for their aims. The dominant figure in the group was undoubtedly the Earl of Essex, whose ambition was to succeed Elizabeth as monarch, and who was eventually beheaded for trying to start a rebellion. Essex, with his constant indecision, is believed to have inspired the character of Hamlet. Other members of the group, together with their associates and enemies, are undoubtedly depicted, in thinly veiled forms, in various Shakespearean characters.

While Shakespeare initially appears to have had considerable sympathy for the aims and methods of the Wilton Group, he seems soon to have realised that root-solutions for human problems would never be achieved by political and military means. He

1. *Shakespeare's Doctrine of Nature*, John F. Danby, Faber, London, 1972

came to view the standards of power and privilege for which they stood with ever-growing revulsion. Instead, lust for power came to be portrayed by Shakespeare as the basic cause of most of humanity's misery and suffering. He saw the solution in feminine wisdom, compassion, and higher love portrayed in such characters as Cordelia, Portia, Volumnia in *Coriolanus*, and Paulina in *A Winter's Tale*. Dominant features of this love are total steadfastness and complete readiness to forgive, whatever the provocation.

Love is not love

Which alters when it alteration finds,

Or bends with the remover to remove:

O, no! it is an ever-fixed mark,

That looks on tempests and is never shaken;

It is the star to every wondering bark,

Whose worth's unknown, although his height be taken.

Love's not Time's fool, though rosy lips and cheeks

Within his bending sickle's compass come;

Love alters not with his brief hours and weeks,

But bears it out even to the edge of doom.[2]

....

2. Sonnet 116, William Shakespeare

The culmination of the Shakespearean oeuvre is the profoundly Gaian vision, derived from Thomas More's *Utopia*, of the remote island in *The Tempest*. This is presided over by a regenerated sage with the moral strength to reject power and unreservedly forgive his enemies. It is significant that one of the spectral figures in the masque in Act 4 represents Ceres, the Roman form of the Greek Earth Mother, Demeter. The mysterious symbiotic forces which convert an ecosystem, such as an island, a forest, or even a mature garden, into an individual entity, in which the whole is more than the sum of its plants, are, in Shakespeare's plays, symbolised by nature spirits and by music. These forces equate with forms of *qi*.

Music has the power to arouse *qi* in the soul of the listener. It can feed the soul as much as plant life feeds the body. With its three basic elements — rhythm, melody, and harmony — it has an essential role to play in the process of holistic development. Any study of the music of peasant or tribal peoples makes clear that music-making must have originally been inspired by the sounds of nature, of Gaia: the rhythms of wind and wave, the melodies of birds, the harmonies of the multiple sounds of the forest.

To me, one of the many musicians with particular significance is Gustav Mahler. He wrote nature-music of great profundity and power at the beginning of the twentieth century, taking inspiration from German folk-song and the glorious scenery of the Austrian Alps, as well as the philosophies of

Goethe, Kant, and Nietzsche. His tremendous Third and Eighth Symphonies are veritable visions of the New Age. The Third has been compared, in its cosmic comprehensiveness and dedication to universal brotherhood, to Beethoven's Ninth.

According to the composer's wife Alma, inspiration for this symphony, known as *The Summer Morning Dream*, suddenly welled up in Mahler as a rush of sound-images, as he stood before his mountain-hut in the Austrian Alps one summer day. His friend, the great conductor Bruno Walter, visited him shortly after the symphony's completion, and described Mahler's personal state: "His whole being seemed to breathe a mysterious affinity with the forces of nature.... At the same time, however – this in the last three movements – I was in contact with the longing of the human spirit to pass beyond its earthly and temporal bonds."[3] The message of the symphony is overwhelmingly hopeful: Walter's name for it was *The Joyful Science*. In the first movement the forces of summer, under the charitable control of the sun, "march in" to impose harmony on elemental chaos. In the last movement, the divine love in the human soul redeems both humanity and the Earth.

Mahler's Eighth Symphony presents a spiritual foretaste of the Gaian Era. Its dominant theme, born out of a period of acute insecurity, anxiety, and doubt, is the redemptive power of the eternal feminine

---

3. *Mahler's Symphonies and Songs*, Banford, 1982, BBC, London

aspects of the one God. The long second movement is a setting of the last scene of Goethe's *Faust*, portraying the Spiritual Quest. The final stage in the growth of spiritual awareness is the vision of the *Mater Gloriosa*, a composite figure conceived by Goethe as a combination of the Virgin Mary and Isis. The final *Chorus Mysticus* ends with the words: "The Eternal Feminine leads us on."

While listening to music is important, there is similar psychic importance in practising music. Music can be therapy for a multitude of ills. It has been recognised for centuries that music is one of the most potent forces for healing body, mind, soul, and spirit. Orpheus, the divinely inspired lyre-player whose melodies could tame wild animals and the dark powers of the underworld, is the archetypal music-therapist. Music played a fundamental role in the Greek therapeutic system, which sought to build up harmony throughout all parts of the human being. In particular, music was valued for its effect in purging, purifying, and uplifting the emotions. As a manifestation of love, it has the power to transmute negative, unhealthy thoughts, feelings, and psychosomatic processes into positive and joyous sensations. It "takes us out of ourselves", helping us to rise from self-absorption, pain, anxiety, and depression into an atmosphere of spiritual enjoyment. Music can also act as an emotional release valve, therefore allowing the internal balance between functions and organs to be restored, therefore leading to increased health.

Music can be a powerful therapy in day-to-day life for us all, for those suffering from temporary attacks of self-doubt to those with more serious depressive illnesses. Patients can experience music as background to massage or treatments, dancing or eurythmics or – most valuable of all – by learning to sing.

There are anatomical grounds for believing that everyone should be a singer. Three pairs of sinuses in the human head correspond to the three registers of the human voice, for which they act as resonators. The singer creates his own instrument inside his body and operates it by a process analogous to Hatha Yoga. Almost the entire body is involved, as well as the mental, spiritual, and emotional faculties. The main focus of effort is the diaphragm, the dome-shaped sheet of muscle which acts as the floor of the chest. As a singer fills his lungs with air, the diaphragm is forced down, converting the chest cavity into a resonating instrument similar to the bag of the bagpipes. Then, through physical effort and intense visualisation, the singer creates a channel from the base of the chest to the top of the skull, activating the vocal chords in the throat and the many muscular and bony cavities that function as resonators. At the same time he concentrates on clear enunciation of notes and words, and on conveying the song's meaning and feeling to an audience. It takes considerable physical and mental effort, learning to be an impersonal channel for the beauty of the words and music.

74

Such intense concentration of physical, mental, emotional and spiritual effort, combined with deep, rhythmic breathing, can be extremely healthy and provide a stimulating sense of spiritual exaltation. My mother, who was urged by her Italian maestro to train as a dramatic soprano, used to say that being in good voice was a sensation akin to flying. At its best, singing is a love-activity, which integrates all parts of the singer's system, from the most spiritual to the most densely material.

In Ancient Greece, as in many peasant and rural societies, almost every activity was accompanied by music. Work songs have rhythms and words that are specially designed to promote energy and provide motivation for specific tasks. Almost every peasant community worldwide has its own wealth of songs, handed down through the generations. Music can have the effect of consecrating every activity with which it is associated, converting the most mundane tasks into acts of worship.

If music is viewed as a form of education of the ear, painting, sculpture, pottery, textile design, and other visual arts constitute education of the eye. Ruskin[4] asserted that the most important aspect of a work of art is always its form. "A pure or holy (whole or healthy) state of anything... is that in which all its parts are helpful or consistent. They may or may

4. Quoted in *Modern Painters, The Law of Help* Vol 5, Part VIII, Chapter 1

not be homogeneous. The highest or organic purities are composed of many elements in an entirely helpful state...In true composition, everything not only helps everything else a little, but helps with its utmost power."

Meditating on a well-composed, harmoniously coloured work of art, or its reproduction, is not only food for the soul, but can also be practical effective eye treatment. Strong forms help to strengthen the eye muscles, while vibrant colours intensify its visual capacity. If you educate your eyes in this way it can help you to foster inner sight, or the capacity for visualisation. Visualisation is creating precise and vivid mental pictures of your aims, or of objects which you desire to heal. As discussed in Chapter 3, you can learn to project these blueprints on to diseased organs, producing a healing, strengthening and regenerating effect.

While landscape painting was a relatively late development in European art, a strong ecological or Gaian element was present in the art of China and Japan from earliest times. Eastern cultures recognise that artistic creation springs from the same source as creativeness in nature. Oriental artists typically try to penetrate behind the obvious external environment to seize the cosmic rhythms that set the currents of life in motion. These life currents are the *qi* which flows along the dragon lines, or leylines, which the Chinese have detected in the landscape for millennia. These currents of energy are the basis of the ancient Chinese art of feng shui, which is the same as the less-recognised Western practice of geomancy.

Binyon maintains that in Oriental art "we do not feel that the artist is portraying something external to himself... The winds of the air have become his desires, and the clouds his wondering thoughts; the mountain-peaks are his lonely aspirations, and the torrents his liberated energies."[5]

Buddhism introduced the compassionate, Gaian figure of Kwanyin, the goddess of mercy, into the art of the Far East. Her form can be found carved into the barren rocks of desolate hillsides in ancient Chinese sculptures, suggesting the yin influences which mitigate the harsher yang forces of nature.

If Mahler's symphonies created attractive and profoundly harmonious sound-pictures of the Age of Gaia, the works of the Russian artist-philosopher, Nikolai Roerich, penetrated to the spiritual essence of the Age. He also prophetically revealed numerous visual images of it. Around the turn of the twentieth century, when Roerich was a young painter, many European artists and writers were already beginning to feel deep anxiety about the rapid growth of industrialisation, fearing that it would lead to wholesale destruction of natural beauty. Roerich shared their fears and his reaction was dynamic, constructive and highly individual. He began to paint idealised views of the Stone Age, when, he believed, human beings

5. *Flight of the Dragon*, Laurence Binyon. Murray, London 1972

77

lived at one with animated nature, teeming with mystic powers. He steeped himself in the past, apparently trying to create an emotional counterpole to the drive of industrialism. He raised the flag for natural beauty and traditional culture, motivated by the conviction that humanity could only regain its soul if it confronted its beginnings in nature. Only then could humanity evolve onto a new plane of peace, harmony, and emotional maturity.

Roerich was joined in his cultural campaign by a group of highly gifted musicians and dancers. This included Diaghilev, Chaliapin, Serge Lifar, and Nijinsky, Stravinsky and Tamara Karsavina, (a virtuoso prima ballerina). Their most sensational collaboration was the Paris premier in 1913 of Stravinsky's ballet *The Rite of Spring*, designed by Roerich. Its vitality seemed to spring from the depths of the Earth.

Roerich's obsession with the distant past led him to become increasingly drawn to the age-old wisdom of the East. He and his wife became devotees of Agni Yoga, the 'yoga of fire' which demands positive action on both the spiritual and material planes; cooperation with the evolution of the cosmos, rather than ascetic meditation or physical exercise alone. In Roerich's case, this action meant dedication to all forms of art, including writing and teaching, as well as painting and designing, because he believed that art must play a key role in the salvation of humanity. Shortly before the October Revolution of 1917, he and his wife left Russia, moving first to Finland and later to the United States. In New York he founded a school for teaching all the arts. Its creed reads like a manifesto for the New Age: "Art will unify all humanity. Art is one – indivisible. Art has its many branches, yet all are one. Art is the manifestation of the coming synthesis. Art is for all.... The gates of the 'sacred source' must be opened wide for everybody, and the light of art will ignite numerous hearts with a new love... How many young hearts are searching for something real and beautiful!"

The Roerichs eventually moved to India and developed a universalistic religious creed, integrating some of the most profound insights of East and West. Beauty and harmony were for Roerich, as for the Ancient Greeks, both the basis and the peak of his religion and practical philosophy.

The power of beauty is desperately needed in today's urbanised, polluted, and uglified Western environment. A vision of beauty is empowering, it enables you to unlock your innate spiritual resources. In any search for a holistic way of life and living you must be open to all the positive forces around you, aesthetic as well as practical. Sometimes you may feel too rushed or stressed to feel moved by a piece of music, or a painting, or a passage of writing; but if you let yourself open up to their positive influences your life will be much the better for it.

Chapter 5

The Inner Ascent

Central to all the great religions and to many systems of philosophy, mysticism, and psychology is the concept of life as a journey, a spiritual quest. My own life has been a journey, sometimes unbelievably hard, and at other times easier and clearer. I have no idea whether I shall ever reach my personal summit, but the journey is always worthwhile and every level I reach represents an affirmation.

Although we each have our own personal quests, they all reflect a universal quest for truth and order, for harmony and a sense of true belonging. Certain writers and thinkers have influenced me throughout my life – Jung, Dante, Bunyan and Tolstoy among others. Their works all feature different aspects of the quest, but project a universal message. Other sources may strike a vibrant chord for other people.

We should all make our own way toward a universal truth, using personal sources of inspiration. Something that is deeply significant for one person may be quite irrelevant for another. But there are certain universal truths about the nature of the search. The object of any spiritual quest is eventually to attain an absolute Truth, and to reach a personal state of wholeness where body, mind, soul, and spirit are fully balanced.

Much of Jung's[1] life was devoted to studying different aspects of the quest[2] – the individuation process – and trying to apply them practically in his work as healer. He discovered that every Age has its own way of aiming for the ultimate goal of the spiritual quest. The true aim of mediaeval alchemy in its genuine form, for example, was to transmute the "base metal" of ordinary human nature into the "gold" of redeemed spiritualised humanity. Different aspects of the quest also feature in many great works of literature, notably Dante's *Divine Comedy*, Bunyan's *The Pilgrim's Progress* and Tolstoy's novel *Resurrection*.

The individuation process is reflected throughout nature in the way every individual organism develops

1. *The Secret of the Golden Flower*, Kegan Paul, London, 1945
2. *The Grail Legend*, Emma Jung and Marie-Louise von Franz, Sigo Press, Boston, 1986

along different lines. There are no two identical plants or animals, let alone human beings. Individuals often feel unable to cope with the realisation of individuality, and a degree of adaptation is absolutely indispensable, since a human being is not only a solitary and isolated creature but also a collective being who requires relationships with others.

According to Jung, a true individual personality consists of a union of these two opposing tendencies. The conflict between them, and their reconciliation, requires the development of consciousness. Individuation is not a simple, straightforward progress, but a long and arduous journey, involving suffering, disappointments, and setbacks. Painful ordeals help an individual gain the practical experience which generates wisdom and spiritual strength.

Tolstoy's novel *Resurrection* is an allegory of individual self-development and a philosophy designed for the New Age. The central character, one of many vividly portrayed individuals, is a self-portrait of the author, and the experiences of this character constitute the background of his philosophy. In *The Kingdom of God is within you*[3] Tolstoy maintained that all evil in the world is due to lack of love, to the substitution of human standards by standards based on wealth, status, and power. This book, with other of Tolstoy's works, had a profound influence on Gandhi.

3. *The Kingdom of God is within you*, University of Nebraska Press, Lincoln, 1984, and other publishers

Together with Dostoevsky's *From the House of the Dead*, Tolstoy's *Resurrection* was a forerunner of a number of novels describing the Siberian experience under Soviet rule, the best known of which is probably Solzhenitsyn's *Gulag Archipelago*. These books, based on real-life events, confirm Tolstoy's thesis that almost intolerable physical conditions can lead to spiritual growth, inner freedom, and even happiness.

When faced with what seems to be an overwhelming concentration of physical force, an individual seeks refuge in his own spiritual resources. He embarks on a journey of inner exploration – and discovers his own indestructible identity, and this discovery brings inner release. The truest freedom is not just absence of external domination and control, but self-fulfilment. It is the realisation that the human being, as the image of God, is equipped with infinite potential for happiness and achievement.

Resurrection was a form of psychological self-treatment and catharsis for Tolstoy. Through it he tried to come to terms with his own moral lapses, above all his callous and unjust treatment of his wife Sonia. It is often possible to interpret other – possibly all – great works of art in similarly existential terms. In order to understand them fully you have to understand the life experiences that created them.

Another notable example is Beethoven's *Eroica* Symphony. The title means 'heroic', derived from Hera, the name of a pre-Hellenic mother goddess. It has been suggested that Hera was originally seen as an embodiment of the fruitful Earth. The hero is a man who seeks psychological roots in the 'soil' of the collective subconscious, taking upon himself the problems of his society or ethnic group and working them out in his own life. The archetypal hero was Herakles (Hercules). His twelve labours represented the ordeals which he overcame in the course of his individual quest, when he discovered his unique identity and eventually attained immortality.

According to one well known story, Beethoven originally dedicated the symphony to Napoleon, striking out the dedication when Napoleon proclaimed himself emperor. But the true hero of the *Eroica* must have been Beethoven himself. This great work can be interpreted as a comprehensive and constructive answer to his traumatic realisation that he had become incurably deaf.

This realisation was the spiritual death that is represented by the funeral march in the symphony's second movement. This original and powerful composition expresses the musician's heroism in accepting the shadow-experience of deafness as a challenge. Beethoven came to understand how facing up to, and overcoming, this challenge was essential to promote his spiritual development.

Every creative individual experiences at some time the phenomenon of inspiration, of intuition, or strongly-directed guidance. On such an occasion it seems as though your brain is taken over by a power outside itself. Then your work, whether writing, painting, composing, sculpting, inventing, or even gardening, starts to flow by its own momentum.

Such creative inspiration is not only experienced by artists. Scientists, including Einstein and Edison, have made similar claims. Nor is the experience of "external intervention" peculiar to men and women of genius. Many people, when faced with awkward problems, have learnt the advantage of "sleeping on" them. You may go to bed with your mind a chaos of facts and ideas, of worries and anxieties. But a good night's rest can lead you to wake with the clear feeling that some co-ordinating power has been at work; everything is in place and the way ahead is obvious – or at least clearer.

It is impossible to define one source of such experiences, although we probably all have our own interpretations. The Ancient Greeks believed that a helpful female agent, a Muse, was responsible. Modern psychologists point to subliminal influences in the personal or collective subconscious. Religious people may claim divine response to prayer, or interpret the assistance according to other strongly-held beliefs. Some Eastern streams of thought, particularly systems of yoga, such as Raja Yoga, claim that the development of this spiritual side, which exists in all of us, can be a precise, controlled, planned and scientific process. "A miracle may or may not happen. But a scientific process must produce the desired result if the right conditions are provided. It is the scientific nature of Yogic techniques which provides the guarantee for success through them.... The Yogic philosophy... considers the whole of the manifested Universe as a cosmos. It declares emphatically that all phenomena within this Universe – superphysical as well as physical – are subject to natural laws which work with mathematical precision."[4]

In some systems of yoga, spiritual development is regarded as a sevenfold process, and, as in Traditional Chinese Medicine, psychophysical forces and organs are involved which are not recognised by orthodox Western anatomy and physiology. Like exponents of TCM, followers of yoga insist that there exists a vast body of reliable, pragmatic evidence, going back several thousand years, for the reality and effective operation of the forces and organs in question.

Whatever the forces underlying the discipline, yoga is a helpful way of focussing on the truth, of moving towards important spiritual insights and promoting spiritual growth. I am sure that I might have been unable either to overcome a wide range of physical problems or to gain spiritual strength in times of apparent adversity without yoga. We should all use whatever is at our disposal in the search for truth and love, gaining inspiration from whatever sources suit our varied temperaments and outlooks.

---

4. *The Science of Yoga*, Professor I.K. Taimni, Theosophical Publishing House, Wheaton, Madras, London, 1961

Chapter 6

The Science of Love

One of the basic laws of Raja Yoga is *ahimsa*, a Sanskrit word meaning non-violence. This has been translated as "an attitude and mode of behaviour towards all living creatures based on the recognition of the underlying unity of life". One very important aspect of yogic practice is the ongoing effort to bring thoughts, words, emotions, and actions into line with this law.

"And gradually this seemingly negative ideal of harmlessness will transform itself into the positive and dynamic life of love, both in its aspect of tender compassion towards all living creatures and its practical form, service."[1]

Of all the characters in past and present history, one individual whom I wholeheartedly admire is Gandhi. Following a tradition thousands of years old, he viewed love as a precise science. In Plato's *Symposium* Diotima is quoted as saying: "This is the right way wherein [a man] should go or be guided in his love: he should begin by loving earthly things for the sake of the absolute loveliness, ascending to that as it were by degrees or steps, from the first to the second, and thence to all fair forms; and from fair forms to fair conduct, and from fair conduct to fair principles, until from fair principles he finally arrives at the ultimate Principle of all and learns what absolute Beauty is."

More than 2,400 years after Plato, Gandhi, who was deeply influenced by the *Bhagavad Gita*, one of the principal textbooks of Raja Yoga, wrote: "Just as a scientist will work wonders out of various applications of the Laws of Nature, even so a man who applies the Law of Love with scientific precision can work greater wonders. For the force of non-violence is infinitely more wonderful and subtle than the forces of Nature, like, for instance, electricity. The men who discovered for us the Law of Love were greater than any of our modern scientists."

In an article in his weekly journal *Harijan* (*Untouchable*) Gandhi affirmed his faith that the law of love would ultimately prevail. He wrote: "Modern

1. Taimni, *op cit in Chapter 5*

science is replete with illustrations of the seemingly impossible having become possible within living memory. But the victories of physical science would be nothing against the victory of the science of life, which is summed up in Love which is the law of our Being."[2]

One of the most important ways in which the science and laws of love are practiced is the compassionate work of healing. The Gospel of the Essenes, which was discovered in both the Library of the Vatican and the Hapsburg Library in Vienna, provides a remarkable Gaian angle to the healing art[3]. It quotes Jesus as saying to a crowd of sick and maimed people who came to him for healing:

"I will lead you into the kingdom of our Mother's angels, where the power of Satan cannot enter... Your Mother is in you, and you in her. She bore you; she gives you life... The blood which runs in us is born of the blood of our Earthly Mother. Her blood falls from the clouds; leaps up from the womb of the earth.... The air which we breathe is born of the breath of our Earthly Mother.... The hardness of our bones is born of the bones of our Earthly Mother, of the rocks and of the stones.... The tenderness of our flesh is born of the flesh of our Earthly Mother; whose flesh waxes yellow and red in the fruits of the

2. 26th September 1936
3. Precise date not given. Translated by Professor Edmond Bordeaux Szekely, C.W. Daniel, Saffron Walden, Essex, 1979

trees, and nurtures us in the furrows of the fields.... The light of our eyes, the hearing of our ears, both are born of the colours and sounds of our Earthly Mother, which enclose us about, as the waves of the sea a fish, as the eddying air a bird.... And he who clings to the laws of his Mother, to him shall his Mother cling also. She shall heal all his plagues, and he shall never become sick. She gives him long life, and protects him from all afflictions; from fire, from water, from the bite of venomous serpents..... Very great is her love, greater than the greatest of mountains, deeper than the deepest seas. And those who love their Mother, she never deserts them."

The Essene Gospel goes on to describe, in great detail, the conditions for natural healing. These conditions have been fulfilled by successful healers throughout every Age.

Gaian healing means making the most of the laws, processes, and resources of nature, and helping others to do the same. That is, in the widest, deepest and highest sense, living naturally and helping others to live naturally. Accounts of the work of natural healers clearly describe how they must heal themselves before healing others. In the Essene Gospel, the laws, processes and resources of nature are described as the Earthly Mother's angels (or Gaia's agents). These clearly include physiological, psychological and psychosomatic processes, those that are recognised by orthodox science and medicine as well as the qi and meridians postulated by Traditional

Chinese Medicine. They also include *prana, kundalini,* and the *chakras* which play fundamental roles in the practice of Hindu yoga. The Essene Gospel emphasises the health-giving resources of nature, of Gaia: clean water, fresh air, sunlight, and the fertile earth; as well as spiritual resources, such as purity, wisdom and truthfulness. It makes clear that love – cohesion, co-ordination, mutual aid – is the first law of Gaia, extolling it in terms similar to those spoken by the disciple Paul: "Though I have faith strong as the storm which lifts mountains from their bases, but have not love, I am nothing". Love is inexhaustible and infinitely enduring.

Many healers express love through their hands, through massage, manipulation, or physiotherapy, or by conveying psychosomatic forces to their patients ʠi or *prana*. Healers are often initially unaware of their powers until a situation arises where they are unconsciously led to use them. One wartime healer who was inspired by love to discover healing power in his hands was British army officer Bruce MacManaway. During the retreat to Dunkirk in 1940, his compassion was aroused by the plight of seriously wounded soldiers who were in great pain but had no access to medical aid. Spontaneously he laid his hands upon them to soothe and comfort them. To his astonishment, he found this had the effect of alleviating pain, arresting bleeding and minimising shock and exhaustion. Realising that he had uncovered a valuable hidden talent, MacManaway felt it his duty to develop the talent to the utmost of his ability. From then on throughout the war, during the Blitz on Britain, during infantry training, and during the campaigns in North Africa and Italy, he took every opportunity that came his way to treat people suffering as a result of accidents, bombing, or gunfire. He helped thousands of people both during and for many years after the war.

Like many people born with visual handicaps, Meir Schneider (see Chapter 3) has exceptional sensitivity in his hands. At an early age he discovered to his joy that he had the power to relieve and even heal people suffering from disabilities that are generally regarded as incurable. These have included muscular dystrophy, Parkinson's disease and multiple sclerosis, as well as many eye defects. Now, at his Center for Self-Healing in San Francisco and at seminars in many parts of the world, he teaches and practises bodywork techniques that he has developed with great success, through incredibly subtle and intuitive use of his hands. Underlying all his work is the basic conviction that "all disease is due to some kind of blockage in the body which interferes with the body's power to heal itself."

The main aim of Schneider's work is, therefore, to locate and dissolve these blockages. He teaches his patients to do this for themselves by developing kinaesthetic awareness, or body consciousness. He shows them how to remove the blockages by massage, manipulation, exercise – or love.

There are examples throughout the world of people similarly blessed with the healing gift who have been able to use this power of love. I have suffered from severe physical problems all my life. Although these problems have sometimes caused me extreme pain and suffering, they have constantly pushed me to search for saner ways of participating in the world. The recent intervention of a healer has lessened my physical difficulties, and may even cause them to disappear altogether. Love really is all-powerful and we should all be open to receive it as well as to give love to others. Society has come to belittle love more and more, to view it as little more than a sentimental notion, but it is much more. Love is a fundamental principle.

Health (as I continually emphasise) is primarily freedom of circulation. There is continuous movement throughout the human system. Blood, lymph, oxygen, nerve impulses, and glandular secretions are in constant flow, carrying hormones, enzymes, minerals, nutrients, and beneficial bacteria to every tissue, to every cell. There they feed, repair and build the body, as well as devouring toxins, wastes and germs, and expelling them through the organs of excretion: the bowels, bladder, lungs, and skin. At the same time conscious and subconscious thoughts and messages are also in constant flow. They direct the muscles to move, the eyes to focus, the ears to hear, the nose to smell, and the nerves to feel – giving orders and information of all kinds. These thoughts travel from our brains throughout the nervous system. In addition, there are undoubtedly spiritual forces at work – *prana* and *qi* – bridging the gaps between our higher and physical selves.

This incessant activity, the innumerable co-ordinated and co-operative interactions between various organs, particles and tissues, forms the essence of life. In order to enjoy abundant energy and vitality, our first aim must be to ensure that the free-flowing forces and elements throughout the system are never blocked or hindered, that our tissues are never clogged. When this happens, our entire internal mechanism slows down, blood and other fluids run sluggishly, messages fail to reach their goals, and acid wastes and toxins accumulate in our joints and elsewhere, where they go sour, rot and cause disease. Blockages are caused not only through lack of exercise and unsuitable foods, but also by shallow breathing and negative, self-absorbed thoughts. Love can be a great dissolver of obstacles, it can be the force that breaks down barriers.

In healing, as in life, love is more than a one-way process. Before healing takes place, any healer will usually try to understand their patient, to build up a whole picture of their background, upbringing, difficulties, essential identity and potentialities for development. This understanding is achieved in different ways, including conversation, meditation or prayer. It leads to genuine love for a patient, understanding of their suffering combined with the desire to help them overcome psychological and physical obstacles to all-round self-fulfilment. If the patient is also open and receptive to trust the healer, then miracles can – literally – happen. Remarkable healing is possible when patient and healer are open to the power of love.

One of the aspects of love that plays a very important part in healing is respect for a patient's God-given identity. For many people, one side of illness that is even more painful than the physical suffering can be the sense of humiliation and inferiority, of being useless and unwanted. This sense often retards or even reverses recovery. Many people experience self-doubt and feelings of inadequacy from time to time, but most of us can at least attempt to hide this from the world around us. The sense of inadequacy is most pronounced when the illness involves disfigurement and is obvious to all. Then the patient feels exposed as an object of disgust. One of the most extreme examples of this is illustrated by leprosy sufferers, who have been feared, isolated and segregated for their illness throughout history.

The Amte family in India fill me with inspiration. They work to cure, relieve and rehabilitate lepers and other severely handicapped people in central and southern India. The Amtes realised from the first that the most important priority in working with lepers was to raise the patients' morale and self-respect. So they take every possible step to find useful, creative work suited to the patients' individual talents, abilities and needs. Their aim is to transform beggars into benefactors, and they often find positive and suitable work in the construction industry. Instead of finding employment for the lepers as unpaid slave labour on building projects – one traditional use for marginal members of any society, the Amtes' encourage their patients to become fully involved in worthwhile community projects. For example, after the severe earthquake at Killari in central India in 1994, Dr Vikas Amte took a team of these skilled rehabilitated lepers to the villages that had been devastated. Following Dr Amte's own designs, they erected high quality, low-cost, environmentally-friendly houses.[5]

Individuals such as the Amtes base all their work on the belief that love really can conquer all. Their practical commitment to solving problems for others is the positive affirmation of this belief.

---

5. For further details see *Forest Gardening*, Robert A de J Hart, Green Books, Bideford, UK, 1991, 2nd ed.1996

Chapter 7

The Organic Community

In order to reach any kind of holistic understanding we must start by understanding ourselves, by caring for ourselves: body, mind, and soul. But holistic development cannot stop with the individual. For complete self-fulfilment, the life of any human being must involve progressive expansion, at least on the psychological plane.

In organic (natural) societies this expansion is facilitated through normal biological means: via the family, extended family, and ethnic community. Organic societies are co-operative systems based on mutual trust, and the expression and satisfaction of mutual needs. These societies can and still do exist in some parts of the globe, typically living close to Gaia and following her laws. Although no human institution is perfect, these remaining organic communities (usually found in "under-developed" countries) provide the most favourable conditions for personal and community growth. They provide models for the new order of human beings who will bring to birth a new world order.

In Western society development has largely come to be motivated by individual greed rather than respect for natural processes and the community. We have moved a long way from organic communities. Moreover, there is a cynical tendency to disregard organic models, and to suggest that problems and conflicts were, or are, just as rife in these idealised societies as in the society we have created. One unhealthy condition of late twentieth century living is the insecurity that so many people feel. This is expressed as alienation and dissociation from whole areas of life, inability to move forwards unless a structure is laid down to be closely followed. Models of more integrated societies can show us how an overall secure and holistic structure, based on the laws of nature and co-operation, permits far greater individual freedom than a fragmented society where each single person feels, ultimately, on their own.

Hundreds of examples of organic communities exist in sociological and anthropological literature, both ideal types and actual examples. One description I recognise, and associate with, comes from Jean

Liedloff, who lived for many years close to nature, and then in intimate contact with Amazonian tribes. Her experiences led her to deduce a principle of Gaian and communal living which she called the Continuum Concept[1]. This way of living was based on what she perceived as a fundamental sense of 'rightness'. Societies following this way of life live according to the principles, laws, and designs of the Earth Mother, of Gaia.

The Continuum Concept was initially inspired by the powerful effect of nature, as seen in a glade in a pine forest in Maine at the age of eight. The glade "had a lush fir tree at the far side and a knoll in the center covered in bright, almost luminous, green moss. The rays of the afternoon sun slanted against the blue-black green of the pine forest. The little roof of visible sky was perfectly blue. The whole picture had a completeness, an all-there quality of such dense power that it stopped me in my tracks. I went to the edge and then, softly, as though in a magical or holy place, to the center, where I sat then lay down with my cheek against the freshness of the moss. 'It is here', I thought, and I felt the anxiety which colored my life fall away. This, at last, was where things were as they ought to be. Everything was in its place... I felt I had discovered the missing center of things, the key to rightness itself."

1. *The Continuum Concept*, Jean Liedloff, Duckworth, London, 1975

This vision remained with her on and off for a number of years, to be suddenly and unexpectedly revived in the "fascinating virginity" of nature at the heart of the Amazonian jungle. There she became aware of "rightness on a grand scale". The jungle "vibrated in its every cell with life, with rightness – ever-changing, ever-intact and always perfect." Later, she experienced the concept in a human context. She spent time as part of the communal life of two Indian tribes, first the Tauripan, and later the Yequana, "truly ecological human beings, as much one with their environment as the animals and plants."

Jean Liedloff defines the human Continuum as "the sequence of experience which corresponds to the expectations and tendencies of the human species in an environment consistent with that in which those expectations were formed." And she adds: "It includes appropriate behaviour in, and treatment by, other people." In other words, the Continuum of an individual human being, in a natural society, can be seen as the centre of a number of concentric circles, corresponding to the family, extended family, community, clan, tribe, nation, humankind and life as a whole. As Jung points out, each one of these biological organisms has its collective unconscious, which influences the individual entity.

Each Continuum has its own expectations and tendencies which spring from a respect for respected precedent. Liedloff's writing contains the positive impression that the co-operative, constructive, integrative laws and processes of Gaia, and the Supreme Cohesive Principle that is God, are far more potent and fundamental facts of life than the forces of pollution and destruction. This is quite opposite from the usual images of endless conflict, corruption and instability so often conveyed by the mass media,

In a Continuum society the development of the individual cannot be torn apart from the development of the various organisms of which it forms part, including Gaia herself. "In each life-form, tendency to evolve is not random, but furthers Continuum interests. It is directed (by mutation and natural selection) at greater stability, ie. at greater diversity, complexity and adaptability."

This biological development, which goes on to include intellectual, emotional and spiritual development, is the exact opposite of what is called "development" in current politico-economic jargon. True development means all-round fulfilment of human potential, involving satisfaction of all our essential needs, physical, mental, emotional, and spiritual. Politico-economic development may be portrayed in an idealistic guise. But it invariably means the imposition by a 'First World' nation of political, financial, industrial, commercial, and military institutions and structures on a 'backward' country. These structures tend to be inappropriate or even harmful to the recipient, and they are also arranged to further the material interests of the donors.

True development, in other words, is from the bottom up. It should begin with analysis of the genuine needs of the people concerned, and should encourage not centralised or international control, but the promotion of small, self-sustaining, self-governing, co-operative communities corresponding (where possible) to natural organisms. These small organic communities provide an individual with the support and stimulus necessary to further his holistic progress towards the unfoldment of his God-given identity. They help him to discover and work out his true vocation, as part of the divine design for a Gaian world order. This blossoming of the individual, and the holistic fulfilment of the latent potential in that individual, is genuine freedom.

When we look at traditionalist peoples, such as certain native Americans and ethnic groups in the Himalayas who are believed to be their distant relatives, evidence of the Continuum is apparent everywhere. It can be seen in the form of harmonious social relationships, mutual supportiveness, poise, dignity, and, in general, readiness to help each other as members of a single family.

One of the most inspiring, comprehensive and detailed pictures of an outstanding Continuum society, describes the remote and mainly Buddhist Himalayan state of Ladakh[2]. Situated on a high and

2. *Ancient Futures*, Helena Norberg-Hodge, 1991, Rider, London

largely barren plateau, in the rainshadow north of the Himalayan watershed, this two thousand year old kingdom of Tartar origin is made up of hardy, self-reliant people. Until the recent advent of Western 'civilisation', they maintained a traditional way of life based firmly on the principle of mutual aid.

Farmers make up the majority of the population, and they share their labour whenever possible, not only because it leads to the most rapid and efficient results, but because they enjoy working with others. The fields at harvest time are filled with men, women and children, reaping and gleaning, talking and singing in time to the rhythm of their work. This may seem a ridiculously romanticised vision to a cynical westerner, but it is the reality for some, and this harmony of relationships and responsibilities maintains a deeply satisfying sense of psychological stability and security. This sense of security was – and still is in rural areas – conveyed into all areas of life. However hard the physical labour, the people remain mentally relaxed. Their emotional health and freedom from stress are derived from deep roots in their soil and society, from networks of inextricable links with each other and their environment.

Buddhist teachings contribute very greatly to the prevalence of the Continuum factor in Ladakhi life. For example, the Sublime Abodes of the Buddha comprise *Metta* (love), *Karuna* (compassion), *Muditha* (joy in the joy of others) and *Upekka* (equanimity). *Metta* includes non-violence and influencing the thoughts of others, especially your opponents, by positive meditation – sending out loving thoughts. *Karuna* demands practical helpfulness and selflessness like the compassion of the Good Samaritan. *Muditha* implies that you should expect no reward from helping others except sharing in their satisfaction. *Upekka* insists that you should remain unmoved either by praise or blame.

Buddha's Four Principles of social behaviour are also highly relevant to the Continuum Concept. These are *Dana* (giving), *Priyavachana* (harmonious speech), *Samanatmatha* (social equality), and *Arthachariy* (constructive work). Dana is usually interpreted to mean the sharing of your time, skills, possessions and energy with your community. *Priyavachana* means neutralising malice and bitterness and promoting mutual respect by emphasising the harmony rather than discord in communications with others. *Samanatmatha* demands the rejection of all distinctions of class and caste – Gautama the Buddha, though a king's son, saw these distinctions as moral outrages. *Priyavachana* indicates that Buddhism accepts what Tolstoy described as the religion of labour, which demands that everyone should, if within their power, satisfy their own needs through physical work.

Through giving, you are not only helping others, but the very act of giving can help you to rise above the downward pull of selfish urges and emotions. This allows your mind to be free to release higher faculties that make the struggle for survival more effective. So giving can have a very empowering effect on the individual who gives, as well as on the person who receives.

The Moslem inhabitants of the Hunza valley in northern Pakistan are near neighbours of the Ladakhis in the Karakoram area. Another Continuum people, they live under the towering guardianship of 25,550 foot Mount Rakaposhi, the "Goddess of the Snows". This race of one-time bandits has adopted a philosophy and policy of total non-violence. They are people of great inner strength, who have been "able to conquer anger, hatred, feverish greed and dangerous ambition and establish a perfect balance of body, mind and spirit."[3] They are believed to be descendants of three soldiers of Alexander the Great, who deserted from his army, married Persian girls, and took refuge from pursuit in that remote mountain valley.

For centuries they subsisted largely by preying on caravans of Chinese traders, who, with their pack-horse trains, ventured to negotiate the narrow tracks across precipitous slopes which link Kashmir to Sinkiang. But, some time over a century ago, the then Mir (king) of Hunza was persuaded by his twelve-year-old son that aggression was contrary to the will

3. Described in *Hunza Health Secrets for Long Life and Happiness*, Renée Taylor, Keats, 1978 and *Yoga, the Art of Living*, Keats, New Canaan, Connecticut, 1992

of God, and he decided that his people must forever renounce the regime of plunder. Since then they have existed largely on the cereals, fruit, and vegetables grown on their intricately terraced slopes, as well as the highly mineralised waters of their glacier streams. Their diet, the water, and their positive outlook on life are all responsible for their incredibly good health and long life, and they are famous throughout the world for both. Unfortunately, even as I write, their way of life is under threat by Westerners who are seeking to exploit their pure water, seeing it as a possible key to longevity.

One crucial test of a Continuum people is the way in which it treats its children. By its very nature, it provides a secure and caring matrix, to which the children can easily conform, and which satisfies their instinctive expectations of what is right. It is understood that young children should never be left alone to suffer from insecurity and isolation, with its fears of the unknown. In Hunza, raising a family is a sacred obligation. Even young children are treated with respect and taught to fulfil useful social roles. Mothers keep their babies with them while they work, and older children take responsibility for younger siblings. Consequently they grow up self-assured, self-confident, emotionally healthy, and genuinely respectful towards their elders. Western cynics may think that such behaviour is coerced, but it appears to spring from an instinctive desire to support and continue the society that fosters them.

The Hopis in the desert country of Northern Arizona provide a good example of another Continuum people dedicated to peace. Despite the continuing encroachment of the western American way of life, despite continuous persecution over the past half-century from government bodies who seek to take their land and therefore their culture, Hopis remain a proud, independent, poised, and steadfast race. Their traditional way of life has been moulded by an environment that is as harsh, in its way, as the very different, mountainous environments of the Hunza and Ladakhi peoples, and in which, like them, they have achieved a high degree of self-sufficiency. Like other ecological people, they are deeply "hefted" (to use the Scottish term) to the land they love, and they have an encyclopedic knowledge of its qualities. They understand the nutritional and medicinal qualities of its plants, and know where to find necessary food and fuel, as well as materials for crafts and building.

True children of Gaia, members of Hopi tribes are spiritually sustained by a profound belief in the forces of nature, and they try to live every aspect of their life and work in complete harmony with nature. Their religious ceremonies are great collective efforts to unite their thoughts, wills, and desires with the powers that govern the growth of crops, the movements of clouds and water, and the health of human beings. While managing to accommodate some of the values of North American society, in order to prevent their young people from leaving to experience a different way of life portrayed as worldly and attractive, traditional Hopi social structure has not changed for centuries. "A Hopi household is a self-directing group, the members of which seem to achieve an automatic co-ordination of their activities. No one exercises authority. The various members seem to fall naturally into a pattern in which the abilities of the individual and the needs of the household are satisfactorily served, a pattern which probably evolved so long ago that it requires no direction and is accepted without question."[4]

At this turning-point in world history, with its conflicts and crime, its diseases and dangers and its still inadequately understood environmental problems, Continuum peoples have much to teach us. Their ways of life illustrate a great deal about both physical and metaphysical techniques of survival.

Every living being, whether human, animal, or even plant, learns a fundamental lesson very early on. Although one initial instinct is self-preservation, which may mean striking out alone in order to survive under difficult or dangerous conditions, there is no point in staying alone. The basic necessity of life is co-operation, or mutual aid. If living beings wish to stay alive, to thrive, prosper, and develop, they soon realise that they must help each other and build a

4. *The Hopis: Portrait of a Desert People*, Walter Collins O'Kane, University of Oklahoma Press, 1990

mutual system of support; they realise that two together can always act more effectively than two separately. They must pool their resources.

The force of synergy is the scientific fact that, when any two or more living beings co-operate, their joint effort is more than the sum of their individual efforts. This is of course particularly obvious when children are the outcome of any male–female yin–yang relationship. The male-female relationship can be highly stimulating and productive in itself, but joint concentration on shared children often enables co-operating parties to rise above themselves in concentrating their joint efforts on caring. There are parallels in many diverse situations, where joint concentration on something mutually produced – whether a living thing, an inanimate object or a joint project – can both have a reconciling effect and cause individuals, groups, or even nations to rise above any petty or long-standing antagonisms in the cause of mutual interest.

Another requirement for survival is continuous positive thinking. Individuals or groups cannot afford to indulge in the luxury of self-pity, malice, carping criticism, or grumbling. These negative modes of thought weaken the mind and lessen the capacity for physical as well as mental control. They lead to mental fragmentation and lack of co-ordination. Positive survival means drawing up clear goals and concentrating all your physical, mental, emotional, and spiritual faculties on attaining your goals.

Your ultimate goal or goals should be based on metaphysical reality, on a picture of the design of God or Gaia for the progressive development of creation. When you know for certain that you are aiming for a genuine goal for the greater good, you will find that you can overcome all sorts of obstacles. When you are acting positively it seems possible to counter even pressing negative forces with mental affirmations of truth. These affirmations, or mantras, must be based on the conviction of Oneness – the basic unity of all life. If you go through life with this conviction, it becomes surprisingly easy to change antagonism into strength and wisdom.

Chapter 8

Humanity and the Landscape

The human impact on the countryside does not have
to mean devastation and ugliness. Under a Gaia-
friendly regime it can mean greater beauty and fertility, an enhancement of natural form, an enrichment
of natural colour, combined with productivity far in
excess of that achieved by "agribusiness" and factory
farming. That is the message of agroforestry, permaculture, landscape architecture, ecological design
and alternative technology.

Sometimes it is tempting to dismiss recent history
as a sequence of unmitigated catastrophes, as a
process of uniform decline from previous peaks of
civilisation, characterised by rejection of humane

111

standards and traditional forms of culture. That is certainly the impression often conveyed by the Western mass media, with its obsession with consumerism and crime, disaster, and depravity. But, largely ignored by the mass media, you can find numerous growing-points of ecological regeneration in many countries, rural invasion of the townscape, constructive and compassionate attitudes towards the natural world. We should not allow ourselves to be disheartened by evidence of decline. Instead, all of us who care about Gaia and her human and animal offspring should concentrate all our efforts on promoting, fostering, encouraging, and linking these growing-points, helping them reach their climax.

Permaculture (permanent agriculture) and agroforestry (agriculture-forestry) are two closely allied systems of growing food and other essential products. They are sustainable schemes which combine trees and other perennials with annual staple crops such as cereals. Both systems are of very ancient origin. Under different names, such as "forest gardening", "home gardening" and "compound farming", they have been practised since time immemorial, especially in tropical areas where ancient civilisations once flourished, such as the Maya-Zapotec area of Mexico and Central America, the Benin area of Nigeria, Kerala in South India, Sri Lanka, and Indonesia.

The systems were given new impetus in the 1970s, when the Australian researcher, Bill Mollison, developed permaculture, and a group of Canadian scientists inaugurated the International Centre of Research in Agroforestry, Nairobi. Since then both systems have spread to reach most parts of the world.

Landscape architecture, the practice of designing natural landscapes combining aesthetic with utilitarian values, was founded in nineteenth century America by Frederick Law Olmsted. Undoubtedly he owed much to the great landscape designers of eighteenth century England such as Capability Brown and Humphrey Repton. The typical park they created, which became a characteristic feature of the English countryside, has been described as a grand didactic poem in the spirit of the Age of Enlightenment. The parks illustrated the conviction that it was the duty of humans to perfect the purposes of nature by the use of their rational faculties.

The aim of ecological design is to create buildings which harmonise with the forms, rhythms and colours of the landscape. The phrase is a modern one, but, like agroforestry, denotes a concept with very ancient origin, as can be seen in the living beauty of many traditional villages and small towns. Significantly, the Ecological Design Association[1] was founded at Stroud in the Cotswolds, a region noted for its villages built of local limestone, where manmade structures are in tune with, and even enhance, the natural environment.

---

1. EDA, The British School, Slad Road, Stroud Glos GL5 1QW

All these new-old systems, techniques, and processes accord with Gaia's basic law of symbiosis – harmony and mutuality. A fundamental feature of symbiosis is respect for diversity. The component parts of a biological organism, such as the human body, are highly individual, highly specialised in form and function. And yet, under normal conditions of health, the end result of all their activities is the integrated wellbeing of the whole.

Gaia abhors uniformity. She does not attempt to impose homogeneity, but encourages every living thing to develop to achieve fulfilment, in its own individual way. Every leaf, every pebble, every living cell is different from all others. Similarly, human beings, in their relations with the land, its flora and fauna, should strive to promote the diversity which is the truest freedom. Their efforts to develop the full potential of the environment can never be truly successful and sustainable if they involve vast structures and mechanisms which suppress and destroy the elements of life. Small is beautiful.

It is upsetting to see homes that are designed as endless straight lines of uniform box-like dwellings. These kind of structures offend on every level, upsetting the human spirit, with its individual loves and inclinations. They inevitably discourage creativity, which is the essence of life. I am sure that they are at least partly responsible for boredom and frustration, even drug-addiction and crime. "Building development" should mean small clusters of cottages, built, so far as possible, from local materials and surrounded by farms, orchards, woods and gardens designed to fulfil the physical and aesthetic needs of their inhabitants. It is just as easy to design well as to design badly, which is apparent in the designs of various enlightened communities. Sustainable developments and ecological villages have been built in Sweden; the new town of Bamberton in British Columbia is a large scale sustainable development; and permaculture villages of Australia also prove that "green design" can be functional and aesthetic. Many smaller developments exist worldwide.

Energy installations need not be vast, obtrusive, dangerous and contaminating structures such as power stations or hydroelectric dams. They can be localised schemes, combining small dams, aerogenerators, biomass digesters and solar devices. Water and sewage schemes should also be localised, and should conform to the latest discoveries about water behaviour and natural effluent disposal. There is no need for sewage farms to be unpleasant smelling eyesores, they can instead be decorative gardens made up of ponds, reedbeds and flowforms — spiral, concrete structures, designed to cause the rhythmic movement of water between cleansing ponds, proved to have an aerating and cleansing effect.

A vast body of knowledge now exists about ecological houses and homemaking, which can easily be accessed rather than seeking instant solutions just because they appear immediately available.

We should make every effort to take the fullest advantage of all precious natural resources, particularly rainfall and the groundwater system. In most Western countries we have come to take supplies of water for granted, but this is a dangerously short-term outlook. We must learn to use every possible means to trap every drop of rain that falls on the local catchment area, and direct it into tanks, reservoirs, swales or underground aquifers. Watershed soils should be treated by keyline and other methods to maximise their water-holding capacity, and woods, coppices and shelterbelts should be planted to facilitate the control of water resources by their root systems.

Whether planning a farm, garden, park, orchard, permaculture plot, plantation or coppice, a designer should make the most of the symbiotic effects of plants upon each other, and between plants and wildlife. In past centuries, and in so-called simpler societies, people were much more attuned to the natural symbiotic processes at work in the plant and animal kingdoms. It was taken for granted that these processes existed. We need to unlearn our modern industrialized ways of looking at mechanistic processes, and relearn the age-old laws of nature, so we can use them to boost the productivity, health, interest, and beauty of any site.

The symbiotic processes at work in a garden have obvious parallels with processes that should be at work in a healthy world. Moreover, humans have an effect on the landscape, but the landscape also effects humanity. The main source of wellbeing in most plants is a fertile soil (though there are a few plants that flourish in impoverished soils). Some plants are especially efficient at enriching the soil, to benefit themselves, their neighbours, and successors, via substances exuded from their roots. The best known of these are the legumes, members of the pea family, which extract nitrogen from the atmosphere with the help of symbiotic bacteria, and fix it in the soil. Members of this family are therefore good companions for the many other plants that require large doses of nitrogen to thrive. Other plants exude soil-conditioning substances such as saponin. Still others exude nutrients which feed the many micro-organisms, beetles, and worms, whose activities drive channels through the soil, helping the circulation of liquids, minerals and oxygen which combine in a healthy soil. Without appropriate channels, blockages occur and elements of fertility are locked up.

Plants need water in order to thrive; this may be conveyed to shallow-rooting plants by the roots of trees, which extract it from spring-veins in the sub-soil. Ground-cover plants may constitute a living mulch, which prevents a soil from drying out at times of drought. Shelter and protection are also vital. Large, coarse, and hardy plants may provide nurse conditions for more tender plants that cannot withstand excessive sunlight, wind, and cold. Many woodland plants thrive in the semi-shade provided by trees and shrubs. Hedges and shelterbelts of trees and shrubs are more effective than fences or walls in protecting young and tender plants from harsh winds, filtering the winds rather than creating solid barriers which can lead to damaging turbulence. Trees and other plants with strong stems can also assist other climbing plants by providing support – mulberry trees, for example, are believed to have an affinity with grapes, so they have traditionally been used throughout Mediterranean countries as supports for grapevines.

There is ample evidence to show that medicinal herbs can have a healthy influence on their plant neighbours as well as on human beings and animals. They seem to do this by excreting essential oils via their roots, and by radiating aromatic gases through their flowers and leaves, which help to deter pests and disease germs.

Nature's symbiotic processes imply more than physical health. Visual vitality is one of the many elements promoting spiritual wellbeing, and plants can provide beautiful and interesting harmonies of form and colour. Many plants also have products and devices (such as fruit, or stocks of nectar and scents) which are highly appealing to wildlife, particularly birds, bees, butterflies, hoverflies, and moths. Apart from giving so much life to the environment, these creatures perform important functions for plants, including the control of pests, pollination and help in distribution of seeds.

You can achieve a special satisfaction from building close relationships with the birds and other wild fauna that haunt your neighbourhood, quite different from the enjoyment of a pet's company. People living close to nature, to Gaia, such as the Hopis, respect the right to life and freedom of all creatures, even of venomous reptiles and insects such as rattlesnakes and scorpions. The reward for this positive non-violent attitude – if fully complied with – is that they are immune from attack.

Many people rightly disapprove of zoos, but animal sanctuaries, where orphaned, neglected, abandoned, ill-treated or sick animals are cared for, have a legitimate role to play in society. They can also illustrate the two-way processes at work between nature and humanity, and the positive effects of one upon the other. One of the most remarkable animal sanctuaries in the world is that established by Prakash Amte, son of humanitarian activist Baba Amte, (described in Chapter 6), in a remote jungle area of Central India.

Amte, who is a doctor, and his wife Mandakini, an anaesthetist, set up a clinic to treat members of the Madi-Gond tribe of aborigines. They are kept very busy treating patients suffering from diseases caused by malnutrition and also from wounds caused by wild animals, including snakes, leopards, and bears. One day Amte met a man carrying a newborn baby fawn, which he intended to take home, kill, and eat. Amte bought it from him. Rearing the tiny thing on the bottle and allowing it to share his and Mandakini's bed at night were the beginning of a love affair with wildlife for both of them. The fawn became an attraction for patients as they waited to see the doctors, and people started bringing other animals they came upon in the jungle. Amte made it known that he did not want any animal deliberately captured for him, but he would be glad to accept any animal that was found in trouble.

The second addition to the sanctuary was a male leopard cub, abandoned by his mother, whom the Amtes named Negal. At the time the couple were looking after a month-old aboriginal baby girl, Aarti, whose mother had died in childbirth. Aarti, Negal, Prakash and Mandakini all shared the same bed for several months and Aarti and Negal grew up as great friends. Negal has remained as tame as any domestic cat, despite the leopard's dangerous reputation.

Over the years the sanctuary's population has grown quite large, including monkeys, bears and crocodiles. The animals are housed in spacious buildings made of mud-bricks with cow-dung floors, and their diet is, as far as possible, vegetarian. Amte claims that the sanctuary has performed a valuable service in teaching the tribespeople to love and respect wild animals, and has therefore contributed to their conservation.

There is evidence that human beings first acquired the qualities and attributes that distinguish them from animals in a natural orchard landscape, possibly in the uplands of East Africa. This landscape provided plenty of the ancestors of the fruit and nuts, green vegetables and herbs which are still recognised to be the foods best adapted to development of the higher human faculties. These would have included a predominance of fruit, leaves, and shoots, high in minerals and other nutrients, drawn by trees and other perennials from deep in the subsoil. Such foods are described in the *Bhagavad Gita* as *satvic* or rhythmic foods in which the life-force is on the upgrade. They are foods which form and nourish brain and nerve-cells and glandular secretions which are sensitive to higher influences and help creative thinking.

Those early, forest-dwelling ancestors of ours, having barely emerged from the womb of Gaia, must have lived permanently in the unitary, undifferentiating state of consciousness described by the French anthropologist Levy-Bruhl as *participation mystique*. He suggested that their minds would have been literally one with those of their animal neighbours, and even of the plants. They would have been guided in many of their actions by the mysterious cosmic currents that guide migrating birds and which enable dogs and cats to find their ways home over hundreds of miles of unfamiliar territory.

Deep natural instincts, and probably the aid of other animals, would have allowed these peoples to understand which of the vast diversity of plant species in their environments were safe to eat or could heal any infrequent ills. Many of these species which were naturally good to eat have disappeared in the course of thousands of years of deforestation.

Such a "primitive" state of consciousness is unaware of a self distinct from other forms of life, still less of a self that is antagonistic to and wishes to dominate and exploit those other forms. That is why, according to worldwide myths of a Golden Age, there was a time when human beings lived in harmony with the most savage beasts.

The psychology of early peoples is described by the philosopher Edward Carpenter as the First State of Consciousness. The Second State is characteristic of our present "civilisation", one in which the self has thrust itself to the forefront and created false barriers of greed, malice, suspicion, and power-hunger that separate it from other forms of life. Self-obsession leads to a sense of isolation that eventually becomes intolerable, causing so much suffering that human beings are eventually forced, by another twist of the evolutionary spiral, into the Third State of Consciousness. This represents the rediscovery of unitary thought, but on a higher plane than that of the First State because it is enriched by the experiences of the intervening "civilisation" phase.

A comparatively small number of people already exist in this Third State today. These are the nucleus of the population of the new world order. Among these are people who live totally non-violent lives close to nature, such as Hindu yogis, Buddhist monks, and members of Amerindian tribes. Stirrings of the Third Plane of Consciousness are now being felt in all parts of the world. They form the irresistible dynamic that has given rise to the Green and organic movements and the numerous campaigns for peace and freedom in almost every country.

One of the many boons of the development of Gaian awareness is the growth of new faculties and new intuitions. With these faculties comes a great appreciation of the beauties of nature and a sense of the oneness of all life. A respected British naturalist, Richard Jefferies, experienced similar feelings to the German mystic Jakob Boehme who claimed to experience the inner qualities of plants. While lying on the Wiltshire Downs Jefferies felt flowers and blades of grass as "exterior nerves and veins", and experienced the "long-drawn life of the earth back to the dimmest past". In his extended prose-poem *The Story of my Heart* he described a state of terrene meditation resembling the prayers for soul-life of the North American Indians.

"With all the intensity of feeling which exalted me, all the intense communion I held with the earth, the sun and the sky... with these I prayed, as if they were the keys of an instrument, of an organ, with which I swelled forth the notes of my soul, redoubling my own voice by their power."

Chapter 9

Practical Solutions –
Make your own Bioregion

A bioregion is the territory providing the life-support system of an organic community or other human society. It defines the geographical, geological, climactic, water, soil, plant, and spiritual conditions that are optimal for the all-round development of a community and its members.

A bioregion also has cultural boundaries: it includes the institutions involved in regional culture, such as schools, colleges, churches, museums, theatres and concert halls.

Until the early decades of the twentieth century, almost all cities and towns throughout the world

124

were the cores of bioregional entities. This changed with the extensive development of heavy transport – trains, large cargo vessels, tankers, juggernaut lorries and jumbo jets. Traditional towns were surrounded by rings of farms, market gardens, orchards, vineyards, forests, quarries, brickworks, and mines, which supplied most of their physical needs. In their turn, the urban centres provided marketplaces, factories and workshops for processing the products of the local countryside, as well as educational and cultural facilities for its inhabitants.

The most serious cause of air pollution in the West is the motor vehicle, while the motorway networks inflict dreadful damage on the countryside. All members of the Green movement should try to use motor transport as little as possible. With this in mind it becomes even more important that families and communities should try and satisfy all or most of their requirements by their own efforts on their own land or within their immediate environment.

Various groups around Britain are now attempting to restore bioregional identity. This means restoring some of the traditional links between a town and its neighbouring countryside, without sacrificing what is best in modern technology: energy and communications networks, building techniques, and labour-saving devices. Rural industries and patterns of life are being revived. There is an increasing interest in organic systems of food production which benefit the physical, social and economic health of townspeople and country dwellers. The reduction of a town's dependence on world trade to meet its basic needs brings significant local and international advantages: vast sums of money are saved, people enjoy fresher food, and less carbon monoxide is emitted to pollute the atmosphere.

The bioregional principle has important world-wide connotations. It is in line with the visions of Gandhi and Schumacher, who saw a new world order based on small, organic groupings, geared to satisfying all the needs of whole human beings, respecting each others' identities, exchanging surpluses and co-operating rather than competing with each other.

Benefits of bioregionalism are particularly relevant to inhabitants of "Third World" countries. In our present consumer culture they are forced to use much of their best land, not to satisfy their own essential needs, but to grow cash crops for export. They work desperately hard, often under terrible conditions, yet are constantly victimised by market forces and financial constraints beyond their control. Most of us buy some imported goods from poorer countries, and we must make sure that these products come via companies with responsible employment practices.

Any group of people who are intending to establish a community should first make a thorough survey of the resources of its chosen area. Every area has specific positive and problematic aspects, and it is important that these qualities are all recognised.

Only then can an area be used to its full potential, with every member gaining the greatest possible benefit. To take a simple example: before planting an orchard or garden, take the time to find out which varieties of tree, bush or herbaceous plant thrive best in the particular area.

One interesting attempt to restore something of Bioregional London has been launched by the Bioregional Development Group at Carshalton in Surrey. The Surrey group tries to apply the principles of permaculture design to all their projects. With the co-operation of local councils and universities, they are devising sustainable, stable, integrated systems for the development of rural resources. Three of the first schemes launched were the Charcoal Initiative, Feasible Fibres and Carshalton Seikatsu.

Britain consumes 60,000 tonnes of charcoal per year, 97 per cent of which is imported, largely at the expense of tropical rainforests and mangroves. The Charcoal Initiative aims to replace imports with home supplies, primarily from 8,000,000 tonnes of low value wood which is said to be going to waste in unmanaged woodland within a 50 mile radius. The effect of this will be to conserve and promote good management of local woods and forests, reviving traditional coppicing techniques.

Feasible Fibres is reviving the cultivation of fibre crops, such as flax and hemp, which historically supplied all Britain's needs for textiles, paper, and rope. This would reduce imports of woodpulp, and

127

cotton; the reasons for reducing imported woodpulp are obvious, and the production of cotton often has devastating effects on the soils and environments of countries overseas. Flax is a traditional fibre; and crops were successfully re-established in several areas of southwest England during World War Two, principally to produce linen cloth, but also for linseed oil. The Surrey group have even produced a collection of clothes made from flax, hemp and other fibres naturally grown in the British climate, including nettles, which were used in Germany to make military uniforms during both world wars. Nettles have the great advantage over flax and hemp of being perennial and (only too) easy to grow.

Carshalton *Seikatsu* (Friends of Organic Farmers) is a consumer co-operative, consisting mainly of mothers concerned about the health of their families and the environment, who buy as much of their food as possible from organic sources with which they have personal contacts. The system is modelled on the hugely successful Japanese *Seikatsu* or CSA (Community Support of Agriculture). This major project involves over 170,000 families operating through a network of small groups. They purchase directly from organic farmers and growers, who gain the advantage of assured markets.

LETS, the Local Exchange and Trading System, is another organisation supporting local bioregions. Launched in British Columbia in the 1980s, it is a way of exchanging goods and services with people in your local community without using money. The system is sweeping across Britain and other countries and has significant potential for the economic life of the whole world, especially in times of crisis. Instead of cash, each local LETS has its own "currency", which is immune to recession, inflation, debt, theft, and scarcity, and carries no interest. Trade is multilateral. Lists are circulated, in which members specify the goods or services they are prepared to offer (or want), and state the number of currency units which they estimate they are worth. Cash figures may also be added, to cover, for example,. out-of-pocket expenses. Transactions are paid for by "cheques" to the number of currency units "spent". The person who receives the cheque is then free to "spend" the amount specified by "buying" goods or services from any other group member. Periodically, members receive a statement of account recording the number of currency units owed or credited.

LETS is an economic system based on mutual trust, friendship, and satisfaction of genuine human needs, rather than greed, or love of power. It also has the bioregional aim of supporting and boosting local economies, keeping wealth local rather than despatching it to distant areas, stimulating local enterprise, making full use of local resources, protecting the environment by cutting down on transport, and re-awakening community spirit.

My own LETS group, Castle LETS in southwest Shropshire, covers a well-defined bioregional area which is largely agricultural, and potentially self-supporting. The area is immortalised by the poet A.E.Housman:

> *In valleys of springs of rivers*
> *By Onny and Teme and Clun,*
> *The country for easy livers,*
> *The quietest under the sun.*

It stretches from the Clee Hills in the east to Clun Forest on the Welsh border, and includes four historic market towns: Ludlow, Bishop's Castle, Clun and Church Stretton. Ludlow is a notable cultural centre and Bishop's Castle has a concentration of people with ecological views. The "currency" is an Onny, named after the small river running through the centre of the area. Varied goods and services are offered, including carpentry and clothes-making, building and babysitting, aromatherapy and accommodation, language tuition and desktop publishing. The Members' agreement states: "Fundamental to Castle LETS is the idea of supporting and building our community by sharing our skills and knowledge for the benefit of all."

While towns or cities are likely to be the cores of most developed bioregions, the fundamental element must be water. At least one watercourse is almost always the dominant feature of any bioregion, and, if there is such a thing as a natural bioregion, it would be a river valley or watershed. A source of drinking water is the first feature that any group of people look for when seeking an area suitable for settlement: an uncontaminated spring, brook, river, or lake. Water is also essential for irrigation and washing, and useful for transport and energy generation.

We all need to be fully aware of the best ways of conserving and preserving water, Gaia's lifeblood. To avoid floods and droughts, it is necessary to control the effect of rainfall on watersheds or catchment areas. Where these are short of trees, have structure-less soils, or surfaces that have been compacted by heavy machinery and/or grazing of sheep or cattle, rainwater cannot be absorbed into the earth. Instead it races downhill, causing erosion and flash-flooding of rivers and streams, and eventually dashing out to sea without benefitting the land. If watersheds are well-wooded and have deep soils with ample under-ground channels, most of the rain remains where it falls, without causing waterlogging, it enhances the fertility of the soil and prevents droughts.

In order to grow annual crops on steep slopes – cereals, vegetables, flax or hemp for example – you must sow them along the contours of the land, rather than up and downhill. This creates a series of ridges or terraces which prevent run-off and erosion. In the Australian keyline system, chisel-ploughs are used to scratch narrow channels across slopes parallel to the contours which pass through 'knickpoints', or 'keypoints', where water collects and forms springs.

131

This spreads water evenly across the slopes so it sinks into the ground. If this system is followed properly, and slopes well prepared, it can lead to dramatic increases in fertility. Sometimes small reservoirs are dug along the 'keylines', which may also be marked out by shelterbelts of trees. Another way to help rainwater to sink into the soil is to dig swales – plant-lined ditches – along contours.

When determining the boundaries of a bioregion, historical, archaeological, religious, and mythological factors should all be taken into account. The most vital bioregions tend to be those that have, for many centuries, been the life-support systems of ethnic groups linked to the land by spiritual affinity, culture and tradition. Notable examples are the territories of Amerindian tribes and the Duthus of Scottish Highland clans. For these people every hill, glen, stream, wood, and rock outcrop – almost every tree – associated with their ancestors is a source of abiding affection, inspiration, and stimulus.

Ethnic identity is regarded by many people today as something to be deplored, as a source of strife and violence, xenophobia, aggression, and the urge to dominate. But there is a wholly positive side to nationality that threatens no-one but enriches world society. Some of the greatest works of art, that have brought joy and inspiration to millions of people, have all sprung from deep in the hearts, collective unconscious, souls, and soils of land-based ethnic communities. These include the symphonies of

Dvòrak and Sibelius, the operas of Janácek and Sallinen, the paintings of Monet, Pissarro, and Turner; the plays of Shakespeare, Goethe, and Euripides; the poems of Dante, Shelley, and Milton; the songs of Schubert and Brahms; the piano music of Chopin and Rachmaninov.

Legitimate love for your own heritage, and the desire for it to be understood and respected, breeds respect for the different but equally valuable heritages of others. The concept of One World does not imply homogeneity, a uniform spiritual waste-land like the prairie farms of agribusiness, but a diverse patchwork quilt of highly individual cultures, traditions, and ways of life, respecting and appreciating each other's unique qualities. These qualities are part of the essential substrata of anyone engaged in the process of holistic self-development.

In my mind there is no doubt that strong emotions become indelibly imprinted on the landscape, just as music became imprinted on wax disks on early gramophone records. There is a high concentration of Iron Age hill-forts in the South Shropshire Hills, two of which, both called Caer Caradoc, are associated with the Celtic warrior king Caradoc, (Caractacus). Caradoc is believed to have made his last stand against the Romans in this area. All of these forts, with their earthen ramparts, sometimes linking rock outcrops, have a very potent atmosphere, and to walk round them is a stimulating and empowering experience. I am not in the slightest superstitious but can testify to this fact. I am convinced that Caradoc still exerts a strong yang influence in this area, an influence which, I feel, has helped to inspire my own creative efforts.

A counterbalancing yin influence seems to come from St. Milburga, the Saxon princess who was the spiritual head of a community of Celtic Christians at Much Wenlock. She is also commemorated by circular structures, but hers are not defensive ramparts like those of the hill-forts. They are instead the outlines of monasteries which she established, which can still be seen in the churchyard walls of village churches which were erected on the Celtic sites. I am quite certain that the Caradoc–Milburga, yang–yin factor contributes to the bioregional unity of the South Shropshire Hills.

Early settlements in many parts of the world were circular in shape, not only because they were felt to be the most secure, but also because they were built to represent the psychologically potent form of the mandála, or sunwheel. The North American Indians' call these structures "Medicine Wheels". They believe these circular forms have a healing effect on those who experience them. A Chippewa-Ojibwa shaman, Sun Bear, has affirmed that Medicine Wheels symbolise the unity and integrity of the universe and the interrelationship of all its component organisms, including human beings.

The ancient science of geomancy, which was most prevalent in China where it is called feng shui, is concerned with determining the most favourable sites for buildings, such as temples, by reference to the currents of terrestrial *qi*.[1] James Lovelock, the scientist who proposed the Gaia hypothesis, admits to being influenced by this way of looking at the world:[2] "Modern medicine recognizes the mind and body as part of a single system where the state of each can affect the health of the other. It may be true also in planetary medicine that our collective attitude towards the Earth affects and is affected by the health of the planet.... I find myself looking on the Earth itself as a place for worship, with all life for its congregation.

"Perhaps because I think this way, I take special comfort from an unusual sacred place which I often visit with my wife Sandy. It is the small church of St. Michael de Rupe, perched upon the central peak of a long extinct Miocene volcano, about half a mile south of the village of Brent Tor in Devon, some ten miles from my home at Coombe Mill.

"At the peak of Brent Tor, on a fine day when the wind comes in from the broad Atlantic bringing clear fresh air, the green dappled fields and woods of Devon stretch out to a far horizon 30 miles away. They form a landscape that looks good, perhaps because the farming is still pre-agribusiness... There

----

1. *Feng Shui*, Master Lam, Gaia Books, London, 1995
2. *Gaia: The Practical Science of Planetary Medicine*, James Lovelock, Gaia Books, London, 1991

is always at the peak of Brent Tor a sense of sacred-ness, as if it were a place where God and Gaia meet. The feeling is intense, like that felt in great cathe-drals, caverns, and on other mountain tops... Brent Tor and places like it have a sense of peace. They seem to serve as reference points of health against which to contrast the illness of the present urban or rural scene."

Brent Tor is one of the most prominent features of the Michael line which runs, almost dead straight, from St Michael's Mount in Cornwall to the Suffolk coast near Lowestoft, incorporating many churches and hills dedicated to St Michael, as well as many dedicated to St Mary. In the Middle Ages St Mary took over the place of St Bride as the Christianised form of Gaia!

Just as water – falling as rain, circulating as rivers, streams, and in underground channels, rising as sap in trees or static as ponds and lakes – constitutes the blood of Gaia, so *qi* is equivalent to her nervous system. Both are equally vital.

We should all be open to acknowledge the influ-ence of a particular area on our personal wellbeing. This is more than an abstract idea, but can have practical as well as emotional effects on our day-to-day life. Any bioregion should contain a good geographical balance of practical and spiritual forces, as well as positive human energy. We should all be proud of our local identity, aware of the way our landscape influences us, and equally of the positive ways in which we may influence the landscape. Once local identity is lost, it is often gone for ever, so we should always try to preserve it, taking full advantage of the unique economic, geographic and cultural potential that it offers.

Local organisations will always carry more genuine power than any monolithic central organisation, and community action is the key towards a positive future. It may sound incredibly banal, but it is true to say that if you take care of your area, it can help take care of you.

Chapter 10

Let's Make a New World

For those who have eyes to see,
there is much reason for hope.

One of the dominant features of the twentieth
century has been the horrifying catalogue of disasters
caused by humans. In view of this, it is only too easy
to adopt a cynical and pessimistic attitude towards
the future. But the profoundest truths of religion,
combined with the latest and most penetrating
insights of science and organic and "alternative"
technologies, demand that we take responsibility to
ensure that positive life-forces prevail. We should
draw up a precise blueprint of a new world order.
And then we must make sure that it is carried out.

A new world will need a new breed of human being. This breed is already appearing. In recent years I have had the privilege of meeting and corresponding with marvellous young people from many countries. The most valuable quality that they share is that they care deeply about the sufferings of their fellow beings and the natural beauty that is being so ruthlessly destroyed. This gives them the courage and determination to make the necessary efforts and sacrifices to reverse the negative trends. I feel I can confidently assert, with gratitude and hopefulness, that they, and what they stand for, are invincible.

The new world order is not being built by formal institutions such as the United Nations, but from the bottom up. Deep and firm foundations are being dug in the soil of societies in many nations. The local aims are as wide and varied as the people involved, but the wider agenda is universal. Gradually a vast network of people power is spreading across the world. New shoots, new growing-points, are appearing all the time from this intricate maze of roots.

One leading academic involved in this process is Dr Robert Muller, the former Assistant Secretary-General of the United Nations, and Chancellor Emeritus of the University for Peace in Costa Rica. Dr. Muller writes: "From all perspectives – scientific, political, social, economic and ideological – humanity finds itself in the kindergarten of an entirely new age, an incredibly promising age, a truly quantum jump, a cosmic event of the first importance, that is perhaps unique in the universe."[1] While admitting that much progress since World War Two has lacked a spiritual dimension, he addresses the world's religions and spiritual traditions, saying: "You, more than anyone else, have experience, wisdom, insights and feeling for the miracle of life, of the Earth and of the universe. After having been pushed aside in many fields of human endeavour, you must again be the lighthouse, the guides, prophets and messengers of the ultimate mysteries of the universe and eternity. You must give humanity the divine or cosmic rules for our behaviour on this planet."

Another leading figure is Thomas Clough Daffern, Director of the International Institute of Peace Studies and Global Philosophy, University of London, and Secretary General of the World Conference on Religion and Peace (UK and Eire). Like Dr Muller, Thomas Daffern also emphasises the fundamental importance of the religious angle. He is editor of the new journal *Love, Compassion and Wisdom*. Introducing this publication in 1994, he claimed that it is "the only academic journal in the world dedicated uniquely to education and research into the positive dynamics of peace building and justice... The purpose of the Love Journal is to assist in the furtherance of a peaceful and just world order, in which armed conflict, violence and war, torture, human

1. *A Source Book for the Community of Religions*, Council for a Parliament of the World's Religions, Chicago, 1993

rights abuse and all the subtle forms of violence and coercion can be replaced by a world culture", characterised by "wisdom, peace, love, compassion, reason, altruism, justice and health."

Daffern is also involved in developing a school of non-violence and conflict resolution for the Gandhi Foundation, whose headquarters in East London are in a hall where Gandhi stayed during his last visit to Britainto negotiate India's future. Behind all Gandhi's campaigns and struggles for freedom, national independence, peace, justice, health, adequate nutrition, good living and working conditions, racial and social harmony – all that is necessary for total human wellbeing – lay a great and visionary Constructive Programme. Gandhi drew up this programme primarily with the circumstances and traditions of his own nation in view, but made clear that its essential features were also applicable to humanity as a whole.

His vision was very much in line with the current Green view of a post-industrial age. His extensive writings contain many concepts, such as "holism" and "conservation of energy", which are strikingly in tune with the most advanced thinking of today. This is because his basic standard in judging every problem, whether political, economic, social, agricultural, or sanitary, had nothing to do with wealth and power but everything to do with human values. He stipulated that the basic unit of the future order of his dreams should be a small, self-governing, self-reliant, and largely self-sufficient community. This was an expression of his conviction that such a group provided the ideal matrix for the all-round, holistic development of the individual man, woman, or child. His entire thinking was essentially constructive, positive, and creative. This was in line with his basic principle of non-violence. The fundamental impulse behind the great campaigns and demonstrations, for which he is best known, was not enmity against the Raj but a desire that the Indian people should develop to the full their innate talents, virtues and potentialities, not only for their own sake but for the sake of humankind as a whole.

Some of Gandhi's most original and practical ideas were contained in his doctrine of Basic Education. Education, in its etymological sense of drawing out or releasing the divine selfhood which exists in every human psyche, should, Gandhi believed, be a life-long process. He perceived Basic Education as a way of life rather than a system for cramming knowledge into the brain, a process of learning through performing useful tasks which aid the development of practical skills as well as wisdom and inner strength. For this purpose, Gandhi advocated the invention of small machines, which could be assembled, maintained, and operated by an averagely intelligent peasant, rather than the giant machines of Western industrialism. Gandhi believed that these tools of large-scale industry enslaved humanity, and at the same time inevitably promoted unemployment and polluted the environment.

Basic Education would not function efficiently in the conditions of vast factories and business enterprises, in which human beings are too often treated as soulless cogs. Gandhi clearly saw that the way for an individual to realise her or his full potential was to live and work in a small co-operative community, where everyone was intimately acquainted with everyone else, recognised and respected each others' talents and identities, had a sense of mutual respon-sibility and enjoyed helping each other. Such groups are the stuff of true freedom, fostering an ideal of lasting peace, leading to individual self-fulfilment and the evolution of a new species of human being which will be the creative impetus for the future.

Everyone knows about Gandhi as a great political leader and non-violent freedom fighter. But he was also one of the profoundest thinkers and prophets of modern times. As a man who strove to live the most exalted religious ideals with every fibre of his being, he will come to be recognised as one of the key fig-ures in the evolution of a new species of humanity and a new world order.

Darwin's theory of evolution by competition and conflict set the pattern for historical development in most parts of the world up to the present day. His theory was challenged with rigorous scientific evidence and research by Petr Kropotkin, a Russian prince who sacrificed a life of privilege and ease in favour of a life of hardship and danger in his search for the truth. In his great book *Mutual Aid*, Kropotkin forcefully presented the view that the basic factor in evolution was not competition but co-operation; but this way of looking at the world has so far had little impact on the powerful manipulators of major trends. The political-economic-military scientific establishment in most countries is still overwhelmingly Darwinian in ethos.

Yet as we draw to the close of one millenium and enter another, I see many encouraging signs which indicate the emergence of a new worldwide alliance capable of challenging these Darwinian models. The new ethos is predominantly feminist and ecological. In accordance with Taoist theory, the long yang period is coming to a close, to be succeeded, in accordance with the rhythmic swing of the cosmic pendulum, by a period which will see the yin forces marching to the fore. One of the important pieces of evidence for this new trend must be the growing acceptance of the Gaia theory.

The most significant scientific discovery at the beginning of the twentieth century was Einstein's theory of relativity. This led to the greatest acts of manmade mass-destruction in history: the atomic bombing of Hiroshima and Nagasaki. But the researches, discoveries, and achievements of Gandhi, Lovelock, Lyn Margulis, Heisenberg, Capra, and many others, are, I am convinced, destined to lead to a phase of unprecedented constructiveness.

Following the explosion of the atomic bombs, Gandhi wrote in his magazine *Harijan* (*Untouchable*):

"There have been cataclysmic changes in the world. Do I still adhere to my faith in Truth and Nonviolence? Has not the atom bomb exploded that faith? Not only has it not done so, but it has clearly demonstrated to me that the twins constitute the mightiest force in the world. Before it, the atom bomb is of no effect. The two opposing forces are wholly different in kind, the one moral and spiritual, the other physical and material. The one is infinitely superior to the other which, by its very nature, has an end. The force of the spirit is ever progressive and endless. Its full expression makes it unconquerable in the world."

"The force of the spirit" is the outstanding evidence of the Truth which was Gandhi's favoured name for God. Faith in Truth, together with persistent affirmations of its reality and power, were the essence of Gandhi's unique technique of *Satyagraha* (Holding to the Truth), the term which he gave to the great mass-demonstrations which were major features of his struggle for national freedom.

Pyarelal, Gandhi's secretary, in his booklet *Gandhian Techniques in the Modern World*[2] describes *Satyagraha* as the opposite of brute force", representing "the power of *Ahimsa* or non-violence which in its positive aspect, is love". It is a form of energy that is "infinitely more subtle, more potent and all-

....

2. *Gandhian Techniques in the Modern World*, Pyarelal Navajivan, Ahmedabad, 1953

145

pervasive" than electricity. "It is governed by laws which are as definite, precise and capable of being objectified as physical laws. It has its science – an exact science – which lends itself to investigation, experimentation and demonstration."

Described in these terms, *Satyagraha* has close affinities with the *qi* which is the basis and essence of Traditional Chinese Medicine (TCM) and the *prana* and other forms of *vata* which play a similar role in the Indian Ayurvedic healing system. Is it possible that all are the same force? Both TCM and Ayurveda are arousing increasing interest in the West. There are so many well-attested cures by both systems that there can be no doubt that the psychosomatic forces that their practitioners claim to work with are actual objective realities – aspects of Truth.

There is One Truth
The most advanced thought of today in both East and West, based on experiments, research, and insights of men and women of outstanding intellect and integrity, points to the fact that there is one Truth. There is one transcendent Reality, and it exists both for science and religion. New Physics and Quantum Theory have moved away from traditions of Newtonian science, to meet the core principle of religion. They postulate a basically unified cosmos, with completely interconnected and interdependent parts which include the observer. There is no place for a detached, unfeeling observer.

Whether a scientist wishes or not, he cannot stand apart from what he contemplates; it is part of himself, it reflects the concepts and images of his own mind. And what he thinks and does affects the object of his thought, and bounces back on himself.

This "revolutionary" revelation of modern science was once an accepted belief. It rejects the cold, mechanistic world-view of Newtonian physics which dominated Western science and economic theory for three centuries, points irrevocably to a supreme cohesive principle as the Creator of the Universe. And the cohesive aspect of the principle is fundamentally incompatible with all theories and practices, including Darwin's, which assert that competition and conflict are basic facts of the universe. There is one principle, one Truth, one Supreme Power, whose aim for every part of His/Her creation is that it should progressively develop and expand its divine potential. Antagonistic factors are the tests and trials which every living organism has to confront, in order to attain the inner strength and experience essential for spiritual progress.

The most powerful of all cohesive forces is the supreme yin quality of compassion, represented by such great religious figures as the Madonna and Kwanyin, the Chinese goddess of mercy. A human being, inspired by compassion in its most acute form, feels that no effort or sacrifice can be too great to alleviate the suffering he sees. All barriers between himself and the sufferer must be broken down; he must pour the very essence of himself into the sufferer's being. This is one way of experiencing the oneness of life postulated by science and religion. The act of compassion itself could be viewed as the spiritual equivalent of an atomic explosion – a great force, or energy, is released which affects all whom it touches. The individual who gave the initial impetus to the process will be unaware of the huge numbers of people touched by the release of energy occurring through his compassionate action.

One of the most significant lessons coming from the understanding of this Truth of Oneness is the knowledge that to bless another is to bless oneself; to harm another is to harm oneself. Therefore humankind must inevitably be forced, sooner or later, to go forward to a new order which benefits life as a whole, an order in which spiritual and emotional wealth takes absolute precedence over material wealth. As many religious reformers such as Gandhi, Kagawa, and Baba Amte have found, the rejects and outcasts of society are often far richer in qualities of spirit, soul and affection than the 'top people' who run today's world.

The yang-forces that have been unleashed in the course of the twentieth century have been ruthless in their wholesale destruction of Gaia's beauty and fertility. One of the supreme tasks that faces the yin-forces – including you and me – is to learn ways to co-operate with and facilitate the Gaian processes of regeneration, rejuvenation, and re-birth. Somehow we have to learn to replace the myriad ecosystems that have been lost with new ecosystems. There is no point in thinking of imitating the spontaneous natural growths that have disappeared, but instead we can rebuild economic systems based on plants which meet human needs. This drive towards sustainability points towards forms of agroforestry.

Many of us look back nostalgically on the landscapes of the past, the wild, unspoiled meadows and woods, the streams and hills that so enchanted us in childhood. Many lovers of the English countryside deeply deplore the uprooting of thousands of miles of hedgerows. But morbid regrets do no-one any good. We must have the courage and vision to look forward to new landscapes, more beautiful, more varied, more fertile, more productive than those of the past. These could be permaculture landscapes, combining aesthetic appeal with conservation of the environment and the production of nourishing foods. New landscapes will contain a great wealth and diversity of food plants, but also trees for beauty and ecological survival; timber trees for building houses and making furniture; fibre plants for spinning, weaving and basketry; biomass plants for energy; medicinal, culinary and aromatic herbs. The varied plant-life should be interspersed with craft-workshops, wind-generators and waterwheels.

If a model Gandhian landscape can be found in the modern world, we should perhaps look at the southern Indian state of Kerala. The state has a great tradition of religious tolerance, which may be partly ascribed to the fact that it contains one of the earliest Christian churches, alleged to have been founded by the apostle Thomas. At the height of Gandhi's great *Satyagraha* campaigns in the 1930s, dedicated groups of young Gandhians and socialists gained a firm foothold in the state, which led to a great land distribution programme, resulting in almost every family owning a small plot of land.

The state now boasts three and a half million forest gardens, which means that most families are self-sufficient in basic necessities. Yet the state is one of the most densely populated in the world, with 747 people per square kilometre. This is more than three times the density of Britain, nearly 30 times that of the USA and more than 300 times that of Australia. The people are not crammed together in tower-blocks, or in squalid and insanitary shanty-towns, but most families live in cottages, half-buried in forest garden greenery. Though Kerala ranks as one of India's poorest states in monetary terms, it is rich in home-grown produce and in culture. The quality of life of its people, especially its women, is acknowledged to be among the highest in the world.

Practices and philosophies such as these, from the so-called Third World, illustrate the ways forward. We all need to recognise fully the interdependence of humanity and nature, and the fact of one Supreme Truth. This provides a guiding principle that we can all follow if we have the will to do so.

Yonder, O my love,
Far out in the wide world,
The wide world, O Mary-Rose
The wide world, Mary-Rose, my love,
Are countless folk,
Sufferers without hope in their need,
Who feel the waves of love,
Surging from our two hearts, O Mary-Rose

APPENDIX

"Sallet herbs" grown in the Forest Garden, as described by John Evelyn in *Acetaria, a Discourse of Sallets*, 1699. These herbs are among many known to have been a regular part of sixteenth and seventeenth century diet in Britain, and Evelyn wholeheartedly recommended that their use should continue. Valued then for their nutritional and therapeutic qualities, but also for their varied and delicate aromatic flavours, they add interesting and health-giving diversity to modern meals.

Alexanders
Moderately hot, cleansin..., Deobstructing, nourishing, and comforting the Stomach.

Balm
Cordial and exhilarating, sovereign for the Brain, strengthening the Memory, and powerfully chasing away Melancholy.

Borage
Hot and kindly moist purifying the Blood, is an exhilarating cordial.

Cress
Moderately hot and aromatick, quicken the torrent Spirits, and purge the Brain.

Endive
Naturally Cold, profitable for hot Stomachs, Incisive and opening Obstructions of the Liver.

Fennel
Aromatick, hot and dry; expels Wind, sharpens the Sight, and recreates the Brain.

Garlic
Tho both by Spaniards and Italians, and the more Southern People, familiarly eaten, with almost every thing, and esteemed of such singular Vertue to help Concoction, and thought a Charm against all Infection and Poyson...we yet think it more proper for our Northern Rustics, especially living in Illiginous and moist places, or such as use the Sea.

Hyssop
Of Faculty to Comfort, and strengthen; prevalent against Melancholy and Phlegm.

Jack-by-the-Hedge
Has many Medicinal Properties, and is eaten as other Sallets, especially by Country People, growing wild under their Banks and Hedges.

Leeks
The Welch, who eat them much, are observ'd to be very fruitful: They are also friendly to the Lungs and Stomach.

APPENDIX

Lettuce
Away Heat, bridle Choler, extinguishes Thirst,
excites Appetite, kindly Nourishes, and above
all refresses Vapours, conciliates Sleep, miti-
gates Pain; besides the effect it has upon the
Morals, Temperance and Chastity. Galen
...says it breeds the most laudable Blood.

Melon
For its transcendent delicacy and flavour,
cooling and exhilarating Nature... Paragon
with the noblest Productions of the Garden.

Mint
Dry and warm, fragrant, friendly to the stomach, powerful against all Nervous Crudities.

Mustard
Of incomparable effect to quicken and revive
the Spirits, strengthening the Memory, expelling
heaviness, preventing the Vertinous Palsie.

Onion
Boil'd, they give a kindly relish: raise Appetite,
corroborate the Stomach, cut Phlegm, and
profit the asthmatical.

Pepper
Of approv'd Vertue against all flatulency pro-
ceeding from cold and phlegmatic Consitutions.

Parsley
Opens Obstructions, is very Diuretic,
yet nourishing.

Purslane
Eminently moist and cooling, quickens
Appetite, assuages Thirst, and is very
profitable for hot and Bilious Tempers.

Rosemary
Soverainly Cephalic, and for the Memory,
Sight, and Nerves, incomparable.

Sage
'Tis a Plant endu'd with so many and wonderful Properties, as that the assiduous use of it is
said to render Men Immortal.

Skirret
Exceedingly nourishing, wholesome and
delicate, of all the Root-Kind, not subject
to be Windy.

Sorrel
Acid, sharpening Appetite, asswages Heat,
cools the Liver, strengthens the Heart; is an
Antiscorbutic, resisting Putrefication.

Succory
More grateful to the Stomach then the Palate.

Tarragon
Tis highly cordial and friendly to the Head,
Heart, Liver, correcting the weakness of
the Ventricle.

BIBLIOGRAPHY

Forest Gardening,
Robert A de J Hart, Green Books, Devon, 1991,
new edition 1996

Ancient Futures,
Helena Norberg-Hodge, Rider, London, 1991

The Life and Art of a Russian Master,
Jacqueline Dieter, Thames and Hudson, London, 1989

Self-Healing, my Life and Vision,
Meir Schneider, Arkana, London, 1987

How to Make a Forest Garden,
Patrick Whitefield, Permanent Publications, UK 1996

Gaia, a new Look at Life on Earth,
James Lovelock, Oxford University Press, 1979

Gaia: The Practical Science of Planetary Medicine,
James Lovelock, Gaia Books, London, 1991

The Grape Cure,
Basil Shackleton, Thorsons, Wellingborough, 1979

The Secret of the Golden Flower,
C G Jung, Kegan Paul, London, 1945

Health from God's Pharmacy,
Maria Treben, Ennsthaler, Austria, 1982

The Spring of Joy,
Mary Webb, Cape, London, 1928

The Science of Yoga,
I K Taimni, TPH Wheaton, Illinois, 1981

Shakespeare's Doctrine of Nature,
John F Danby, Faber, London, 1972

The Grail Legend,
Emma Jung and Marie-Louise von Franz,
Sigo Press, Boston, 1986

The Flight of the Dragon,
Laurence Binyon, Murray, London, 1972

BIBLIOGRAPHY

The Kingdom of God is within you,
Leo Tolstoy, University of Nebraska Press, Lincoln, 1984

Raw Energy,
Leslie and Susannah Kenton, Century, London, 1984

The Continuum Concept,
Jean Liedloff, Duckelt, London, 1975

Hunza Health Secrets,
Renée Taylor, Keats, Connecticut, 1978

Yoga, the Art of Living,
Renée Taylor, Keats, Connecticut, 1992

Gandhian Techniques in the Modern World,
P Pyarelal, Navajivan, Ahmedabad, 1953

The Elements of Native American traditions,
Arthur Verolius, Element Books, Dorset, 1993

A Source Book for the Community of Religions,
Council of a Parliament of the World's Religions,
Chicago, 1993

The Hopis, Portrait of a Desert People,
Walter Collins O'Kane, University of Oklahoma Press,
Norman, 1953

Green Inheritance,
Anthony Huxley, Gaia Books, London, 1991

The Natural Garden Book,
Peter Harper, Gaia Books, London, 1994

The Feng Shui Handbook,
Master Lam Kam Chuen, Gaia Books, London, 1995

The Book of Ayurveda,
Judith H Morrison, Gaia Books, London, 1994

The Natural House Catalog,
David Pearson, Simon and Schuster Fireside, New York, 1996

Gaia Atlas of Planet Management,
ed. Norman Myers, Gaia Books, London 1994

INDEX

INDEX

INDEX

ALSO PUBLISHED BY GAIA

For a complete list of titles published by Gaia Books, write to or telephone Gaia Books,
20 High Street, Stroud, Gloucestershire, GL5 IAS Tel: 01453 752985 Fax: 01453 752987

EARTH TO SPIRIT
In search of natural architecture

David Pearson
£11.99
ISBN 1 85675 046 9

In the past, buildings expressed an ancient consciousness, a harmony between people, land and cosmos that linked Earth to Spirit. David Pearson, author of *The Natural House Book*, explores new architecture that honours old traditions, yet uplifts them with current ideas - from home and garden to community design.

ECOYOGA
Practice and meditations for walking in beauty on the Earth

Henryk Skolimowski
£10.99
ISBN 1 85675 071 X

Incorporating ancient wisdom, classical harmony, and the ideas of new science, this beautiful book of practices and meditations puts us all in touch with our roots. The author takes us on a practical and fulfilling journey of spiritual renewal, showing us ways to live in harmony with the Earth.